BOY SCOUTS ON A LONG HIKE

or

To the Rescue in the Black Water Swamps

ARCHIBALD LEE FLETCHER

1st WORLD
LIBRARY
Literary Society

Boy Scouts on a Long Hike

Archibald Lee Fletcher

© 1st World Library, 2006
PO Box 2211
Fairfield, IA 52556
www.1stworldlibrary.com
First Edition

LCCN: 2006907674

Softcover ISBN: 1-4218-2418-3
Hardcover ISBN: 1-4218-2318-7
eBook ISBN: 1-4218-2518-X

Purchase *"Boy Scouts on a Long Hike"*
as a traditional bound book at:
www.1stWorldLibrary.com/purchase.asp?ISBN=1-4218-2418-3

1st World Library is a literary, educational organization
dedicated to:

- Creating a free internet library of downloadable ebooks

- Hosting writing competitions and offering book
  publishing scholarships.

1ˢᵗ World Library Literary Society

Giving Back to the World

"If you want to work on the core problem, it's early school literacy."

- James Barksdale, former CEO of Netscape

"No skill is more crucial to the future of a child, or to a democratic and prosperous society, than literacy."

- Los Angeles Times

Literacy... means far more than learning how to read and write... The aim is to transmit... knowledge and promote social participation."

- UNESCO

"Literacy is not a luxury, it is a right and a responsibility. If our world is to meet the challenges of the twenty-first century we must harness the energy and creativity of all our citizens."

- President Bill Clinton

"Parents should be encouraged to read to their children, and teachers should be equipped with all available techniques for teaching literacy, so the varying needs and capacities of individual kids can be taken into account."

- Hugh Mackay

CONTENTS

CHAPTER I

THE BOYS OF THE BEAVER PATROL

"They all think, fellows, that the Beaver Patrol can't do it!"

"We'll show 'em how we've climbed up out of the tenderfoot class; hey, boys?"

"Just watch our smoke, that's all. Why, it's only a measly little twenty-five miles per day, and what d'ye think?"

"Sure Seth, and what's that to a husky lot of Boy Scouts, who've been through the mill, and wear merit badges all around? Huh! consider it as good as done right now!"

Half a dozen boys who wore khaki uniforms, were chattering like so many magpies as they stood in a little group on an elevation overlooking the bustling Indiana town of Beverly.

Apparently they must have been practicing some of the many clever things Boy Scouts delight to learn, for several of the number carried signal flags; two had pieces of a broken looking-glass in their possession; while the tall lad, Seth Carpenter, had a rather sadly stained blanket coiled soldier fashion about his person, that gave off a scent of smoke, proving that he must have used it in communicating with distant comrades, by means of the smoke code of signals.

Besides Seth there were in the group Jotham Hale, Eben

Newcomb, Andy Mullane, Fritz Hendricks, and a merry, red-faced boy who, because of his German extraction, went by the name of "Noodles Krafft."

The reader who has not made the acquaintance of these wide-awake scouts in previous volumes of this Series will naturally want to know something about them, and hence it might be wise to introduce the members of the Beaver Patrol right here.

Eben was the official bugler of Beverly Troop. He had been made to take this office much against his will, and for a long time had the greatest difficulty in getting the "hang" of his instrument, so that his comrades guyed him most unmercifully over the strange medleys he used to bring forth when meaning to sound the various "calls." But of late Eben seemed to have mastered his silver-plated bugle, and was really doing very well, with an occasional lapse excepted.

Andy was a Kentucky boy, but outside of a little extra touch of pride, and a very keen sense of his own honor, you would never know it.

Seth was the champion signal sender, and delighted to study up everything he could discover concerning this fascinating subject.

Fritz, on his part, chose to make an especial study of woodcraft, and was forever hunting for "signs," and talking of the amazing things which the old-time Indians used to accomplish along this line.

As for good-natured Noodles, if he had any specialty at all, it lay in the art of cooking. When the boys were in camp they looked to him to supply all sorts of meals that fairly made their mouths water with eagerness to begin operations long before the bugle of Eben sounded the "assembly."

Last of all the group, was Jotham Hale, a rather quiet boy, with an engaging face, and clear eyes. Jotham's mother was a

Quaker, or at least she came from the peace-loving Friends stock; and the lad had been early taught that he must never engage in fights except as a very last resort, and then to save some smaller fellow from being bullied.

On one occasion, which no one in Beverly would ever forget, Jotham had proven that deep down in his heart he possessed true courage, and grit. He had faced a big mad dog, with only a baseball bat in his hands, and wound up the beast's career right on the main street of the town, while everybody was fleeing in abject terror from contact with the animal.

Because in so doing Jotham had really saved an old and nearly blind veteran soldier from being bitten by the terrible brute, he had been adjudged worthy to wear the beautiful silver merit badge which is sent occasionally from Boy Scout Headquarters to those members of the organization who have saved life at great peril to themselves.

But Jotham was not the only one who proudly sported a badge. In fact, every one of the eight members of the Beaver Patrol wore a bronze medal on the left side of his khaki jacket. This had come to them because of certain services which the patrol had rendered at the time a child had been carried away by a crazy woman, and was found, later on, through the medium of their knowledge of woodcraft.

Of course there were two more boys connected with the patrol, who did not happen to be present at the time we find them resting on their way home after a rather strenuous afternoon in the open.

These were Paul Prentice, the patrol leader, and who served as acting scout master when Mr. Alexander was unable to accompany them; and "Babe" Adams, the newest recruit, a tenderfoot who was bent on learning everything connected with the game.

They had gone home a little earlier than the rest, for reasons that had no connection with the afternoon's sport, each of them having a pressing engagement that could not be broken. "Babe" had been nick-named in the spirit of contrariness that often marks the ways of boys; for he was an unusually tall, thin fellow; and so far as any one knew, had never shirked trouble, so that he could not be called timid in the least.

"No use hurrying, fellows," declared Seth, as he flung himself down on a log that happened to be lying near the edge of a little precipice, marking the abrupt end of the shelf which they had been following, so that to descend further the scouts must pass around, and pick their way down the hillside.

"That's so," added Jotham, following suit, and taking great care not to knock his precious bugle in the least when making the shift; "for one, I'm dead tired after such a hard afternoon. But all the same, I want you to know that I'm in apple-pie condition for that long hike, or will be, after a night's rest."

"What d'ye suppose made Mr. Sargeant offer a prize if the Beaver Patrol could walk to Warwick by one road, and back along another, a distance of just an even hundred miles, between sunrise of four days?" and Fritz looked around at his five comrades as though inviting suggestions.

"Because he's fond of boys, I reckon," remarked Andy. "They tell me he lost two splendid little fellows, one by drowning, and the other through being lost in the forest; and when he learned what sort of things the scouts practice, he said he was in favor of encouraging them to the limit."

"Well, we want to get busy, and show Mr. Sargeant that we're going to give him a run for his money," said Seth.

"We've all seen the cup in the window of the jewelers in town, and it sure is a beauty, and no mistake," added Jotham.

"Don't anybody allow himself to think we can't cover that hundred miles inside the time limit. You know how Paul keeps telling us that confidence is more'n half the battle," Fritz went on to say.

"You pet we want dot gup, undt we're yust bound to get der same," observed Noodles, who could talk quite as well as any of his mates, but who liked to pretend every now and then, that he could only express himself in "broken English," partly because it pleased him and at the same time amused his mates.

"We're right glad to hear you say that, Noodles," declared Seth, with a wink in the direction of the others; "because some of us have been afraid the hike might be too much for you, and Eben."

"Now, there you go again, Seth," complained the bugler, "always imagining that because I seldom blow my own horn -" but he got no further than this, for there broke out a shout, from the rest of the boys.

"That's where you struck it right, Eben!" cried Seth, "because in the old days you seldom did blow your own horn; but I notice that you're improving right along now, and we have hopes of making a champion bugler out of you yet."

"Of course that was just a slip; but let it pass," remarked Eben, grinning in spite of the fact that the joke was on him. "What I meant to say was that because I don't go around boasting about the great things I'm going to do, please look back on my record, and see if I haven't got there every time."

"Sure you have," admitted Seth, "and we give you credit for bull-dog stubbornness, to beat the band. Other fellows would have thrown the bugle into the bushes, and called quits; but you kept right along splitting our ears with all them awful sounds you called music. And say, if you can show the same kind of grit on this long hike we're going to try, there ain't any doubt but what we'll win out."

"Thank you, Seth; you're a queer fish sometimes, but your

heart's all right, underneath the trash," observed Eben, sweetly; and when he talked like that he always put a stop to the other's teasing.

"How about you, Noodles; d'ye think you're good for such a tough walk?" asked Fritz, turning suddenly on the red-faced, stout boy, who was moving uneasily about, as though restless.

"Meppy you don't know dot me, I haf peen practice on der quiet dis long time, so as to surbrize you all," came the proud reply. "Feel dot muscle, Seth, undt tell me if you think idt could pe peat. Gymnastics I haf take, py shiminy, till all der while I dream of chinning mineself, hanging py one toe, undt all der rest. Meppy you vill surbrised pe yet. Holdt on, don't say nuttings, put wait!"

He put on such a mysterious air that some of the boys laughed; but Noodles only smiled broadly, nodded his head, and made a gesture with his hand that gave them to understand he was ready and willing to let time vindicate his reputation.

"Hadn't we better be moving on?" remarked Andy.

"Yes, the sun's getting pretty low in the west, and that means it must be near supper time," said Fritz, who was the possessor of a pretty brisk appetite all the time.

"Oh! what's the use of hurrying?" Seth went on to say, shifting his position on the log, and acting as though quite content to remain an unlimited length of time. "It won't take us ten minutes to get there, once we start; fifteen at the most. And I like to walk in just when the stuff is being put on the table. It saves a heap of waiting, you know."

"That's what it does," Eben echoed. "Because, if there's anything I hate to do, it's hanging around while they're finishing getting grub ready."

"Here, quit walking all over me, Noodles!" called out Fritz, who had coiled his rather long legs under him as well as he could, while squatting there on the ground.

"I haf nodt der time to do all dot," remarked the German-American boy, calmly, "idt would pe too pig a chob. Oh! excuse me off you blease, Fritz; dot was an accident, I gif you my word."

"Well, don't stumble across me again, that's all," grumbled the other, watching Noodles suspiciously, and ready to catch him at his tricks by suddenly thrusting out a foot, and tripping him up - for Noodles was so fat and clumsy that when he took a "header" he always afforded more or less amusement for the crowd.

It was not often that Noodles displayed a desire to play tricks or joke, which fact made his present activity all the more remarkable; in fact he was developing a number of new traits that kept his chums guessing; and was far from being the dull-witted lad they had formerly looked upon as the butt of all manner of practical pranks.

While the scouts continued to chat, and exchange laughing remarks upon a variety of subjects, Noodles kept moving restlessly about. Fritz felt pretty sure that the other was only waiting for a good chance to pretend to stumble over his legs again, and while he pretended to be entering heartily into the rattling fire of conversation, he was secretly keeping an eye on the stout scout.

Just as he anticipated, Noodles, as though discovering his chance, lurched heavily toward him. Fritz, boylike, instantly threw out a foot, intending to simply trip him up, and give the other a taste of his own medicine.

Well, Noodles tripped handsomely, and went sprawling headlong in a ludicrous manner; but being so round and clumsy he rather overdid the matter; for instead of simply rolling there on the ground, he kept on scrambling, hands and legs shooting out every-which-way; and to the astonishment and dismay of his comrades, Noodles vanished over the edge of the little precipice, close to which the scouts had made their temporary halt while on the way home!

Archibald Lee Fletcher

CHAPTER II

HELPING NOODLES

"Oh! he fell over!" shouted Eben, appalled by what had happened.

"Poor old Noodles! What if he's gone and broke his neck?" gasped Jotham, turning a reproachful look upon Fritz.

"I didn't mean to go as far as that, fellows, give you my word for it!" Fritz in turn was muttering, for he had been dreadfully alarmed when he saw poor Noodles vanish from view in such a hasty fashion.

"Listen!" cried Andy.

"Hellup!" came a faint voice just then.

"It's Noodles!" exclaimed Fritz, scrambling over in the direction of the spot where they had seen the last of their unfortunate chum.

"Oh! perhaps he's gone and fractured his leg, and our family doctor, meaning Paul, ain't along!" groaned Eben.

All of them hastened to follow after the eager Fritz, and on hands and knees made for the edge of the shelf of rock, from which in times past they had sent many a flag signal to some scout mounted on the roof of his house in town.

Fritz had more of an interest in discovering what had happened to the vanished scout than any of his comrades. Possibly his uneasy conscience reproached him for having thrust out his foot in the way he did, and sending poor Noodles headlong to his fate.

At any rate he reached the brink of the descent before any of the rest. They unconsciously kept their eyes on Fritz. He would serve as a barometer, and from his actions they could tell pretty well the conditions existing down below. If Fritz exhibited any symptoms of horror, then it would afford them a chance to steel their nerves against the sight, before they reached his side.

Fritz was observed to crane his neck, and peer over the edge of the shelf. Further he leaned, as though hardly able to believe his eyes. Then, when some of the rest were holding their breath in expectation of seeing him turn a white face toward them, Fritz gave vent to a hoarse laugh. It was as though the relief he felt just had to find a vent somehow.

Astounded by this unexpected outcome of the near-tragedy the others hastened to crawl forward still further, until they too were able to thrust out their heads, and see for themselves what it was Fritz seemed to be amused at.

Then they, too, chuckled and shook with amusement; nor could they be blamed for giving way to this feeling, since the spectacle that met their gaze was comical enough to excite laughter on the part of any one.

Noodles was there all right; indeed, he was pretty much in evidence, as they could all see.

In falling it happened that he had become caught by the seat of his stout khaki trousers; a friendly stump of a broken branch connected with a stunted tree that grew out of the face of the little precipice had taken a firm grip upon the loose cloth; and since the boy in struggling had turned around several times,

Archibald Lee Fletcher

there was no such thing as his becoming detached, unless the branch broke.

"Hellup! why don't you gif me a handt?" he was shouting as he clawed at the unyielding face of the rock, while vainly endeavoring to keep his head higher than his flying heels.

While it was very funny to the boys who peered over the edge of the shelf, as Noodles would have an ugly tumble should things give way, Andy and Seth quickly realized that they had better get busy without any more delay, and do the gallant rescue act.

Had Paul been there he would have gone about it in a business-like way, for he was quick to grapple with a problem, and solve it in short order. As it was a case of too many cooks spoiling the broth, one boy suggested a certain plan, only to have a second advanced as a better method of getting Noodles out of his unpleasant predicament.

Meantime the poor fellow was kicking, and turning, and pleading with them not to go back on an old chum, and leave him to such a terrible fate.

"Der rope - get quick der rope, undt pull me oop!" he wailed.

"That's so, boys, Noodles has struck the right nail on the head!" cried Seth. "Here, who's carrying that rope right now?"

"Noodles has got it himself, that's what!" exclaimed Eben.

"Did you ever hear of such rotten luck, now?" demanded Seth.

"Hold on!" interrupted Andy, "seems to me I remember seeing him lay something down over here. Let me look and find out. Whoop! here she is, boys! That's what I call great luck. Seth, suppose you see if you can drop the loop over his head."

"Pe sure as you don't shoke me, poys!" called out the dangling object below, in a manner to prove that he heard all they said.

"Get it over his feet, Seth; then we can yank him up. He won't mind it for a short time. Some of his brains will have a chance to run back into his head that way," suggested Eben.

"Make quick, blease!" wailed the unhappy scout, who was growing dizzy with all this dangling and turning around. "I hears me der cloth gifing away; or else dot dree, it pe going to preak py der roots. Hurry oop! Get a moof on you, somepody. Subbose I want to make some squash pie down on der rocks?"

But Seth was already hard at work trying to coax that noose at the end of the dangling rope to fall over the uptilted legs of the unfortunate scout.

"Keep still, you!" he shouted, when for the third time his angling operations were upset by some unexpected movement on the part of the struggling boy. "Think I c'n lasso a bucking broncho? Hold your feet up, and together, if you want me to get you! There, that's the way. Whoop-la!"

His last shout announced sudden success.

Indeed, the loop of the handy rope had dropped over the feet of Noodles, and was speedily drawn tight by a quick movement on the part of the operator.

The balance of the boys laid hold on the rope and every one felt that the tension was relieved - that is, every one but Noodles, and when he found himself being drawn upward, with his head down, he probably thought things had tightened considerably.

As the obliging branch saw fit to let go its tenacious grip about that time, of course Noodles was soon drawn in triumph over the edge of the shale, protesting more or less because he was scratched in several places by sharp edges of the rock.

"Hurrah for Scout tactics; they count every time!" exclaimed Eben.

Fritz was unusually solicitous, and asked Noodles several times whether he had received any serious hurt as a result of his strange experience. The German boy felt himself all over, grunting several times while so doing. But in the end he announced that he believed he was all there, and beyond a few minor bruises none the worse for his adventure.

"Put you pet me I haf a narrow escape," he added, seriously. "How far must I haf dropped if dot pully oldt khaki cloth gives vay?"

"All of twenty feet, Noodles," declared Andy.

"Dwenty feets! Ach, petter say dree dimes dot," asserted Noodles. "I gives you my word, poys, dot it seemed I was on der top of a mountain, mit a fine chance my pones to preak on der rocks pelow. Pelieve me, I am glad to pe here."

"I hope you don't think I did that on purpose, Noodles?" asked Fritz, contritely.

The other turned a quizzical look upon him.

"Tid for tad, Fritz," he remarked, "iff I had nodt peen drying to choke mit you meepy I might nodt haf met with sooch a shock. Petter luck nexdt time, hey?"

"I don't know just what you mean, Noodles, blest if I do," remarked Fritz, with a puzzled look on his face, "but I agree with all you say. This practical joke business sometimes turns out different from what you expect. I'm sure done with it."

But then, all boys say that, especially after they have had a little fright; only to go back to their old way of doing things when the shock has worn off. And the chances were that Fritz was far from being cured of his habits.

"How lucky we had the rope along," ventured Jotham, who was coiling up the article in question at the time he spoke.

"I always said it would come in handy," remarked Eben, quickly and proudly, "and if you stop to think of the many uses we've put that same rope to, from yanking a fellow out of a quicksand, to tying up a bad man who had escaped from the penitentiary, you'll all agree with me that it's been one of the best investments we ever made."

"That's right," echoed Seth, always willing to give credit where such was due.

"Ketch me ever going into the woods without my rope," declared Eben.

"Well, do we make that start for home and mother and supper right now; or are we going to stay here till she gets plumb dark?" asked Fritz, impatiently, moving his feet out of the way every time anyone approached too closely, as though possessed by a fear lest he be tempted to repeat his recent act.

"Come on, everybody," said Eben, making a start, "I refuse to hang out a minute longer. Seems like I c'n just get a whiff of the steak a sizzling on the gridiron at our house; and say, when I think of it, I get wild. I'm as hungry as that bear that came to our camp, and sent us all up in trees like a covey of partridges."

"If you're as hungry as that after just an afternoon's signal practice, think what'll happen when we've been hiking all day, and covered our little forty or fifty miles?" suggested Andy, chuckling.

"Oh! come off, Andy, you don't really mean that, do you?" called out Eben over his shoulder. "I'm good for twenty-five miles, I think; but you give me a cold feeling when you talk about fifty. And poor old Noodles here will melt away to just a grease spot, if the weather keeps on as warm as it is now."

"Don't let him worry you, Eben," sang out Seth. "I heard Paul telling how at the most we might try for thirty the second day, so as to get ahead a bit. But what is going to count in this test is regularity - keeping up an even pace each day of the four. And chances are we'll own that fine trophy by the time we get back to Beverly again."

"Didn't I hear something about our having to register at a lot of places along the way?" asked Jotham.

"Yes, I believe that's a part of the game," replied Seth. "It's only right, just to prove that we haven't cut across lots, and shirked any. Mr. Sargeant and the two members of the committee mean to wait up for us at each station, and kind of keep an eye on us. I guess they want to encourage us some, too, when we come in, dusty and tired and feeling pretty near fagged out.

"Some of the other fellows, Steve Slimmons, Arty Beecher, and two more, who expect to start our second patrol in the fall, wanted to go along with us; but Mr. Sargeant preferred to limit it to just the Beavers. He said we were seasoned scouts by this time, while the other fellows might be called tenderfeet; and it would be a pity to run chances of losing the prize, just because one of them softies fell down."

Fritz offered this explanation, and somehow at mention of Steve Slimmons' name a slight smile could be seen flitting across more than one face. For well did the scouts remember when this same boy had been accounted one of the toughest lads in all Milltown, as that part of Beverly across the railroad tracks was called.

At that time he had been called "Slick" Slimmons, and in many ways he deserved the name, for he was a smooth customer. But circumstances had arisen, as told in a previous volume of this series, whereby Steve had gone through a rather serious experience, and had his eyes opened to the fact that in leading such a wild life he was carrying the heavy end of the log.

He had broken with the tough crowd of which he had been a member up to then, and now was hand in glove with Paul Prentice and his scouts, in fact considered himself a member of Beverly Troop.

The active lads found little trouble in negotiating the descent leading down to level ground. Even Noodles had become many times more agile than before he donned the magical khaki of the scouts; for the various duties that had to be performed from time to time by every member of the patrol had done wonders for the slow moving German-American boy.

With their goal now in sight, the six scouts started off at a lively pace. If any of them felt in the least bit tired he was evidently determined not to show it to his comrades, or any one they might happen to meet on the road leading to Beverly. Pride is a great thing at certain times, and helps ride over many difficulties.

So, in due time they separated, each fellow heading toward his own home. And the last words they called back to each other were in connection with the great hike upon which they expected to start on the following morning, which would be Tuesday.

Many anxious looks were cast upward toward the blinking stars that night, and speculations indulged in as to the probable kind of weather that would be doled out to them while on the road.

And more than one scout lay awake long after he went to bed, trying to lift the curtain that hid the future, just a little way, so as to get a peep of what was waiting for the Beaver Patrol, but of course without the least success.

CHAPTER III

THE GENTLE COW

"Paul, how do we hold out for the third day on the hike?"

"Yes, and Paul, please let us know just how much further you expect to coax the leg weary bunch on today? Not to say that I'm tired; but then I know Noodles, and another scout not far away right now, are grunting like fun every little rise in the road we come to," and Seth gave his head a flirt in the quarter where Eben was anxiously gripping his bugle, as if in momentary expectation of getting a signal from the patrol leader to blow the call that would signify a halt.

"It's only four o'clock, fellows," began the acting scoutmaster.

Dismal groans sounded; but with a smile Paul went on to add:

"We've already made our twenty-five miles since sun-up, just this side of Warwick; but it's a fine day, and I did hope we might hang on a little while further, so as to cut down our last day's hike a few miles. It's always the hardest part of the whole thing, the finishing spurt. But of course, if any of you feel played out we can call it off right now."

Eben and Noodles braced themselves up at this, and tried to look as though they had no calling acquaintance with such a thing as fatigue.

"Oh! I'm good for a couple more miles, I guess," declared the former.

"Make idt tree, undt you will see how I holdt oudt!" proudly boasted the stout boy, who spent half his time mopping his red face; for the day had been a pretty warm one, so Noodles, who had to carry a third again as much weight as any of his companions, thought.

"Bully boy!" exclaimed impulsive Seth, "didn't I say they had the sand to do all we tried. You never would have believed Noodles here could have covered the ground he has. Scouting has been the making of him, as it will of any feller that cares to set his teeth together, and just try real hard."

"I suggest then," went on Paul, his face beaming with pleasure, "that we take a little rest right here, say of half an hour; and then march along again for three miles, as near as we can guess. And if we do that, fellows, it leaves only twenty more for the last day."

"I reckon that silver trophy is as good as won," remarked Andy Mullane.

"Barring accidents; and you never can tell when something may happen," added wise Seth.

"Then I hope it will be to you, and not to me," said Eben, who was rubbing his shin at a place where he had bruised it earlier in the day.

"Have we got enough grub along to last out?" queried Fritz.

All eyes were turned toward Noodles, who generally looked after this part of the business when they were abroad, either camping or tramping.

"I wouldn't say yes, if Fritz he puts der crimp in dot appetites off his," was what the cook announced, gravely.

"Then we'll see to it that he gets no more than his regular ration after this," Paul declared, pretending to look severe.

"Huh! that makes me feel real bad right away, let me tell you, fellers," Fritz remarked, touching his belt line with a rueful face. "However do you think I can fill up all this space here with just one ration? It's different with some of the rest of the bunch; take Noodles for example, he hasn't got room for more'n half a ration. I speak for what he can't make way with."

"Say, there's a chance right now for you to fill up ahead of time!" exclaimed Eben, as he pointed through the fence; and looking, the scouts saw a cow standing there, placidly chewing, her cud, and evidently watching them curiously as she attended strictly to business.

"Sure," Fritz went on to say, quickly, getting to his feet, "she's got plenty of rations, quarts and quarts of fine rich milk. I've got half a notion to step in there, and see how it tastes. See here, if I tied a nickel or a dime in a piece of paper, and attached it to her horn, wouldn't that be all right, Paul? Ain't scouts got a right to live off the country as they hike through, 'specially if they pay for what they take?"

"Well, if it was a case of necessity, now -" began the scoutmaster.

"It is," broke in Eben, who for some reason seemed to want to egg Fritz on, "our comrade's plumb near starved, you know, and we're talking of cutting his grub allowance down to half. But I don't think he's got the nerve to fill up on nice rich fresh milk, that's what. Some people talk pretty loud, but when you pin 'em down, they say they didn't mean it."

Of course that finished Fritz. If he had been joking before, he now took the matter in a serious light.

"Huh! that remark don't hit me, Eben," he said, disdainfully, "If it was a ferocious old bull I might hesitate about trespassing on his field, but a gentle cow, whoever knew one to act ugly? Here goes, after I've tied up this nickel in a piece of paper, with a string to it, to fix it on Sukey's horn. Anybody else feel milk thirsty? Don't all speak at once now, because I'm first."

Apparently no one else was hankering after fresh milk just then; at least none of the scouts gave any indication of meaning to accompany the bold invader.

"If you're really intending to go over the fence and try the milk supply," suggested Paul. "I'd advise you to leave that red neck scarf that you're so proud of wearing, behind you, Fritz."

"Yes, that's so," broke in Seth, "cows, as well as bulls, don't fancy anything red, I've been told. Better leave it with me, Fritz."

"Huh, think I ain't on to your little game, Seth Carpenter," declared the other, making no move to take off the necktie in question, "don't I know that you've always wanted that scarf? Ain't you tried to buy it off me more'n a few times? Not much will I let you hold it. That tie stays by me. If the poor old cow don't like it, she can do the next best thing. Now, watch me get my fill, fellers. Milk is the staff of life, more'n bread; and I always did like it fresh. Here goes."

He clambered up on the top of the fence, while all the other scouts watched to see how the operation turned out.

"Take care, Fritz," warned Eben, solemnly, "she's got her eye on you, all right, and she's stopped chewing her cud too. P'raps she may turn out to be a hooker; you never can tell about cows. And chances are, she's got a calf up in the barn. You see, a cow is always ugly when she thinks they're agoin' to steal her calf away, like they did lots of other times."

"Oh! rats!" sneered the valiant Fritz, drawing his staff over with him, so as to get a purchase on the ground within the field, and ease his intended jump.

"Listen, Fritz," added Jotham, "see that little enclosure just back of where she stands? Looks like it might have been fenced off to protect some fruit trees or something. Well, if I was in your boots now, and she made a jump for me, I'd tumble over that same fence in a hurry. A cow's got horns the same as a bull, and you'll be sorry if ever she tosses you."

But Fritz had evidently made up his mind, and would not allow anything to deter him. The more the other scouts threw out these hints the stronger became his determination to carry his clever scheme to completion. And when he said he was fond of fresh milk Fritz only told the truth; though the chances were he would never have accepted such a risk only for the badgering of Eben and Seth.

Using his long staff in a dexterous way he dropped lightly to the ground, and immediately started to walk toward the spot where the cow stood.

She had raised her head a little, and appeared to be observing his coming with certain suspicious signs.

"Go slow, Fritz; she don't like your looks any too much!" warned Paul, who had climbed to the top of the rail fence, the better to see what happened.

Perhaps Fritz himself may have felt a little qualm just about that time, for the actions of the cow were far from reassuring; but he was too proud to show anything that seemed to savor of the "white feather" before his chums, especially after making all the boasts he had.

And so he kept grimly on, even if his knees did begin to knock together a little, when he actually saw the cow suddenly lower her head, and throw up the dirt with those ugly looking short horns, to one of which he had so recently declared he meant to secure the coin he would leave, to pay for all the milk he expected to consume.

Paul had called out once or twice, words of warning. He also suggested that it would be wise for the adventurous one to turn back; because, if appearance went for anything the animal had a bad temper, and would be apt to give him more or less trouble.

But that had no effect on Fritz, who, having embarked on the venture, did not mean to back down until absolutely forced to do so.

And so the other five scouts, ranged along the fence, watched to see what would happen. Perhaps their hearts were beating just a little faster than ordinary; but if so, that was not a circumstance to the way Fritz felt his throbbing like a trip hammer, even while he kept steadily moving ahead.

He started to utter what he meant to be soothing words, as he approached the gentle bovine. He had heard farmers talking to their cows when starting to do the milking act, and thought it the proper caper. But Bossy must have finally made up her mind that this trespasser had a suspicious look, and meant to carry off the little calf that could now be heard calling away off beyond a rise where a farm house and stable evidently lay.

Suddenly she lowered her head, and started toward Fritz. Frenzied shouts arose from those who were watching the proceedings from a safe distance.

"Run, Fritz! she's coming!" bawled one.

"Remember the fence over there, Fritz, and what I told you!" cried Jotham.

Fritz did not take the trouble to reply. He could hardly have done so even had he so desired, for just then he was most actively employed.

At the time the cow made her abrupt plunge toward him the scout could not have been more than thirty feet away. He was

Archibald Lee Fletcher

wise enough to realize that should he attempt to make a wild dash for the fence surrounding the field, the active four legged animal would be able to overtake him before he could get half way there. And as the one way left to him Fritz jumped to one side, in order to avoid contact with those cruel-looking black horns.

His first act was one of impulse rather than anything else; he just sprang to one side, and allowed the animal to go surging past, so close that he could have easily reached out his hand, and touched her flank, had he chosen to do so.

Of course she would quickly realize that her attack had been a failure, and recovering, turn again to renew it. He must not be on the same spot when that time came. And as there was no better opening offered than the enclosure mentioned by Jotham, he started for the same, with the cow in full pursuit, and his chums shrieking all sorts of weird advice.

So close was the angry animal behind him that at first Fritz could not take the time to mount that fence. He chased around it, and as if accepting the challenge, Bossy did the same, kicking her heels high in the air, and with tail flying far in the rear.

Fritz managed to keep a pretty good distance ahead of his pursuer, and as there did not seem to be any particular danger just then, some of the boys allowed their feelings of hilarity to have full swing, so that peals of riotous laughter floated to the indignant ears of the fugitive.

Indeed, Eben laughed so much that he lost his hold, and fell into the meadow; but it was ludicrous to see how nimbly he clambered up again, as though fearful lest the cow take a sudden notion to dash that way, changing her tactics.

Meanwhile Fritz was laying his plans looking to what he would call a coup. When he had gained a certain distance on the circling cow, so that he would have time to scramble over the fence, he hastened to put this scheme into operation.

Fritz had dropped upon the ground, and was evidently panting for breath. At any rate, the boys, perched like a lot of crows on the distant fence, could see him waving his campaign hat rapidly to and fro, as though trying to cool off after his recent lively experience.

"Look at the old cow, would you?" burst out Eben, "she sees him now, I tell you! Say, watch her try and jump that fence, to get closer acquainted with our chum. Oh! my stars! what d'ye think of that now; ain't she gone and done it though?"

While the bugler of Beverly Troop was speaking, the angry cow made a furious dash forward. Eben had naturally imagined she meant to try and follow Fritz over the fence but he was wrong. There was a terrific crash as the head of the charging beast came in contact with the frail fence; and the next thing they knew the cow had thrown down an entire section, so that no longer did any barrier separate her from the object of her increasing fury.

CHAPTER IV

IN ALABAMA CAMP

Fritz was no longer sitting there taking things comfortably, and cooling himself off by using his hat as a fan.

With the terrific crash the scout was on his feet, ready for further flight, as he saw the head of the cow not ten feet away from where he stood.

This time he made straight for another section of the fence, and passed over it "like a bird," as Seth declared. But evidently fences had little terror for the aroused cow, since she immediately proceeded to knock down another section in about the space of time it would take to read the shortest riot act ever known.

This prompt act again placed her on the same side as the fleeing Fritz. The loud shouts of his chums warned him of her coming on the scene again, even if that suspicious crash had failed to do so.

Fritz was becoming used to clambering over fences by now; in fact it seemed to be something like a settled habit.

The cow saw his lead, and went him one better, for a third crash told how the poorly constructed fence had gone down before her rush, like a pack of cards in the wind.

All the while Fritz was changing his location. He calculated that if only he could hold out for say three more "climbs," he would be in a position to make a run for the border fence, which was made much more stoutly then the division one, and would probably turn back even a swooping bull.

After it was all over, Fritz would demand that his comrades give him full credit for his cunning lead. Meanwhile he was kept as busy as any real beaver; getting first on one side of the crumpling fence, and then on the other; while the cow kept on making kindling wood of the barrier.

Paul took advantage of the animal's attention being wholly centred upon Fritz, to run out upon the field, and pick up the cast-off staff of the busy scout. His intention at the time was to render all the assistance in his power; but discovering that Fritz was rapidly approaching a point where he could work out his own salvation, the scoutmaster thought discretion on his part warranted a hasty departure, unless he wished to take the place his comrade vacated.

The boys on the fence were shouting, and waving their hats, and doing all manner of things calculated to attract the attention of the "gentle cow," and cause her to ease up in her attack; but apparently she was not to be bought off so cheaply, and meant to pursue her advantage to the bitter end.

Then came the chance for which the artful Fritz had been so industriously working, when he made one more fling over the remnant of the enclosure fence, and upon reaching the outside, galloped away toward the road as fast as his legs could carry him.

Of course the cow chased after him again as soon as she had knocked down another section of fence; but Fritz seemed to have pretty good wind, considering all he had been through; and he showed excellent sprinting powers that promised to put him among the leaders at the next high school field sports exhibition.

And the other five scouts gave him a hearty cheer when they saw him nimbly take the high fence on the bound, with those wicked horns not more than five feet in his rear.

They soon joined the panting one, who greeted his mates with a cheery grin, as though conscious of having done very well, under such distracting conditions.

"But you've yet to know whether that milk is as rich as you hoped?" remarked Paul, smilingly, as he handed Fritz his staff.

"And chances are, you went and lost that blessed nickel you meant to tie to one of gentle Bossy's horns; what a shame, and a waste of good coin!" said Seth, pretending to be very much disappointed.

"Huh! getting off pretty cheap at that!" grunted Fritz. "Ketch me tryin' to milk any cow that's got a calf up in the barn. I'd rather face two bulls than one like her. Don't ever mention milk to me again; I know I'll just despise the looks of it from now on. Whew! but didn't she mean business; and if ever those sharp horns had got attached to me, it would have been a hard job to break away."

"If you feel rested, and have changed your mind about that same splendid milk," remarked Paul, "perhaps we'd better be getting along now. Three miles - why, Fritz, I wouldn't be much surprised if you covered all of that in the little chase you put up. All you needed to beat the record for flying was a pair of wings."

Fritz was wonderfully good-natured, and they could not make him angry. When other boys were apt to scowl and feel "grouchy," Fritz would come up smilingly after each and every round, ready to take punishment without limit.

And so they continued to walk along the road, chatting among themselves as cheerily as footsore and weary scouts might be expected to do when trying to encourage each other to further exertions.

Every step really meant a good deal to their success, for in the course of ten minutes Paul declared that another mile had been duly covered.

When they saw another cow inside a fenced enclosure the boys tried by every argument they could devise to tempt Fritz to try his hand once more, but he steadfastly declined to accept the dare.

"Say what you like, fellers," he remarked firmly, "me and cows are on the outs, for this trip anyway. It's somebody else's turn to afford amusement for the bunch. I've sure done my duty by the crowd. Let me be, won't you? Tackle Seth there, or Babe Adams. I happen to know that they like milk just every bit as much as I do. Water's good enough for me, right now; and here's the spring I've been looking for a long while."

At that they all hastened to discover some spots where it was possible to lap up a sufficient supply of the clear fluid.

This cooling drink seemed to invigorate the boys, so that when they started off again it was with a somewhat quicker step, and heads that were held up straighter than of late.

It enabled them to reel off another mile without any great effort.

"Only one more, and then we've just got to let up on this thing," said Paul.

"I really believe you're getting tired of it yourself, Mr. Scoutmaster?" ventured one of the boys, eagerly; for if Paul would only confess to this, they felt that they could stand their own weaknesses better.

"And that is no joke," laughed Paul, frankly. "You see, I haven't been hardening my muscles as much lately as when the baseball season was in full swing. But with two miles placed to our account, we shouldn't be much worried about how things are coming out. Will we try for that last mile, boys? It's for you to say!"

He received a unanimous shout of approval, which announced that the others were of a united mind. And so they kept along the road though some steps lagged painfully, and it was mainly through the exertions of the mind that the body was whipped into obeying.

Finally Paul turned to Eben, and made a quick gesture that the bugler was waiting for, since he immediately raised the shining instrument to his lips, puffed out his cheeks, took in a tremendous breath, and gave the call that was next to the "fall in for supper" signal, the most popular known to the scouts.

"Alabama! Here we rest!" cried Seth, turning aside into the woods after Paul, who evidently had his eye on a certain location, where he meant to pitch the third night's camp.

"That's a good idea," remarked Andy, always quick to seize upon anything that gave a hint concerning his beloved South, "let's call this Alabama Camp!"

"Put it to a vote," called out Fritz, "all in favor of the same say aye; contrary no. The ayes have it unanimously. Hurrah for Alabama Camp. Seems like that's a good restful name; and I hope we sleep right good here; for most of us are pretty well used up."

"Don't mention that same above a whisper," warned Seth, "because we've got two awfully touchy chums along, who're always carrying chips on their shoulders when it comes to the subject of being knocked out. Say, Paul, did you know about this camp site before; because it's the dandiest place we've struck on the big hike?"

"Just dumb luck," replied the other, shaking his head in the negative. "I thought it looked good this way, when I called for a halt. And you're just about right, Seth; it does fill the bill great. Here's our spring of clear cold water; and there you have a splendid place to start your fire, Jotham. Now, let's throw ourselves down for a little while, and then when we feel rested, we'll get busy doing things."

All of them were only too glad to do as Paul suggested. And when another ten minutes had slipped past, Jotham struggled to his feet to wearily but determinedly gather together some material with which to start a blaze.

When he had it going Noodles realized that it was now up to him to start getting some supper cooking. They had come in very light marching order, since Paul realized that if they hoped to win that lovely prize he must not load any of the boys down with superfluous burdens.

As a rule they depended on the farmers to supply them with such things as they needed, chiefly eggs and milk. The former they had along with them, several dozen eggs in fact, purchased from an obliging farmer earlier in the afternoon, and fortunately carried in other knapsacks than that of Fritz, who would have smashed the entire supply, had he been in charge of the same at the time of his exciting adventure with the cow.

Upon putting it to a vote they decided that they could just as well do without any milk for one night; especially after Fritz had shown them how difficult it sometimes was to accumulate a supply.

Of course a coffee pot had been brought along, for somehow a camp must always seem like a dreary desert without the delicious smell of boiling coffee at each and every meal that is prepared.

So Noodles made a grand big omelette, using sixteen eggs for the same, and the two frying pans that had been strapped, one

Archibald Lee Fletcher

to each pack of a couple of scouts.

Besides this they had some cheese and crackers, which would help fill the vacuum that seemed to exist an hour after each and every meal. Several potatoes for each scout were duly placed in the red ashes of the fire, and jealously watched, in order that they might not scorch too badly before being thoroughly roasted.

On the whole, there was no reason for being ashamed of that camp supper. Everything tasted just "prime," as several of the boys took pains to say; for they were artful enough to know that by showering words of praise upon the cook, they might secure his valuable services for all time to come, because Noodles was open to flattery.

And what was better still, there was an abundant supply for all of them, regardless of the difference in appetites; Fritz was not stinted in the least, for he actually declined a further helping, and had to be urged to clean out the pan just to keep "that little bit of omelet from being wasted."

Having no tent along, and only a couple of dingy old blankets which they expected to use for sending smoke signals, should the occasion arise, the scouts were compelled to resort to more primitive ways of spending the night than usual. But then Paul had shown them how to sleep with their heads away from the fire; and he also arranged to keep the small blaze going during the entire night, since it was apt to get pretty chilly along about two in the morning.

All these things had been arranged on the first night out, so that by this time the boys were pretty well accustomed to the novel way of sleeping. And on the whole they had taken to it fairly well, no one complaining save when the mosquitoes annoyed them in one camp near the water.

An hour after supper had been disposed of some of the boys were already beginning to nod drowsily. And when fellows are just dead tired it seems a sin to try and keep them awake, especially when there is no need of it.

So Paul announced that those who wanted to could turn in, while the rest were enjoined to keep quiet, doing their talking in whispers, so as not to disturb the sleepers; just as if the discharge of a six pound cannon close by would bother those weary scouts, once they lost themselves in the dreamland of Nod.

Babe Adams had just stepped over to get a last drink at the near-by spring, when the others were surprised to see him come tearing back again, evidently in great excitement.

"Paul, come over here with me, and you can see it!" he called out.

"See what?" demanded the scoutmaster, at the same time climbing to his feet.

"Looks like some farmhouse might be afire; because you c'n see the red flames jumping up like fun!" was the thrilling announcement made by the tenderfoot scout.

CHAPTER V

A HELPING HAND

"It's a fire, all right!" announced Paul, after he had taken a good look.

"No question about that," declared Seth, who was right on the heels of the others, for you could never keep him quiet when there was anything going on, because he always wanted to be "in the swim."

"Yes, either a house, or a barn ablaze," remarked Eben, sagely.

"Might be only a hay stack, you know," suggested Jotham.

"Don't burn like that to me; I seem to see something of a building every now and then, when the flames shoot up," Paul went on to remark, for he was always discovering things upon which to found a reasonable theory.

"How far away does it lie, dy'e think, Paul?" asked Andy.

"Not more than half a mile, I should say," came the reply.

"Just my idea to a dot," Jotham admitted.

"Why, you c'n even hear the crackle of the flames, whenever the night wind happens to blow this way," Babe Adams asserted; and they all agreed with him, for the same sound had come to their ears also.

"We might help the poor old farmer, if we only happened to be closer," Eben said, in the goodness of his heart.

"And if we didn't feel so bunged-up tired," added Andy.

Somehow the scouts began to show signs of nervousness. Those might seem like pretty good excuses to some fellows; but when a boy becomes a scout he somehow looks at things in a different way from in the old days. No matter how tired he may be, he eagerly seizes on a chance to be useful to others; to do some good deed, so as to experience the delightful glow that always follows a helpful act.

"Say, how about it?" began Jotham.

"Could we be useful if we did manage to trot over there, Paul?" Andy demanded.

"I'm sure we might," answered the scoutmaster, firmly; "and if we're going, why, the sooner we make a start the better. Seconds count when a house or barn is on fire. I feel pretty well rested, speaking for myself; and half a mile each way oughtn't to do us up. We're scouts on a long hike, and able to do lots of things that other fellows wouldn't dare attempt."

"Take me along, Paul!" cried Jotham.

"And me!"

"Hope you won't forget that I'm ready to be in the bunch," Seth exclaimed.

In fact, there was not one out of Paul's seven companions who did not vociferously inform the leader of the patrol that he was a subject for the draft.

"You can't all go," decided Paul, quick to decide; "and as two fellows ought to stay and look after camp while the rest are off, I'll appoint Noodles and Eben to that duty."

Groans followed the announcement.

"Oh! all right, Paul; just as you say," remarked the bugler, after giving vent to his disappointment in this manner; "we'll keep guard while the rest of you are having a bully good time.

"Perhaps something will happen along here to let us enjoy ourselves."

"If you need help let us know it," Paul called back, for he was already moving off in the direction of the fire, followed by the five lucky scouts.

"How?" bellowed Noodles; "do we whoop her up, Paul?"

"Sound the assembly, and we'll hurry back," came the answer, as the pack of boys disappeared in the darkness of the night.

They kept pretty well together, so that none might stray. Consequently, when one happened to trip over some log or other obstacle that lay in the path he would sing out to warn his comrades, so as to save them from the same trouble.

With such a bright beacon ahead there was no trouble about keeping on a direct line for the fire. And all the while it seemed to be getting more furious. Indeed, what with the shouts that came to their ears, the bellowing of cattle, and whinnying of horses, things began to get pretty lively as they approached the farmyard.

Presently they seemed to break out from the woods, and reach an open field. Beyond this they could plainly see the fire.

"It's a barn, all right!" gasped Jotham, immediately.

"Yes, and they seem to be afraid that the farmhouse will go, too," added Andy.

"They're throwing buckets of water on it, sure enough," sang out Babe Adams.

Now some of the boys could easily have outrun their mates, being possessed of longer legs, or the ability to sprint on occasion; but they had the good sense to accommodate themselves to the rest, so that they were still in a squad when drawing near the scene of the excitement.

A man and a woman seemed to be about the sole persons visible, and they were laboring like Trojans to keep the fire from communicating to the low farmhouse that was situated close to the burning barn.

The six scouts must have dawned upon the vision of the sorely pressed farmer and his wife almost like angels, for the pair were nearly exhausted, what with the labor and the excitement.

"Buckets - water - let us help you!" was what Paul exclaimed as they came up.

Cows were running this way and that, bellowing like mad, as though half crazed.

What with frightened chickens cackling, and hogs grunting in their near-by pen, the scene was one that those boys would not forget in a hurry.

"In the kitchen - help yourselves!" the farmer said, pointing as he spoke; and without waiting for any further invitation the scouts rushed pellmell into the rear part of the house, where they seized upon all sorts of utensils, from a big dishpan, to buckets, and even a small tin foot bath tub.

A brook ran close to the barn, as Paul had learned with his first comprehensive glance around. This promised to be a most fortunate thing for the would be fire-fighters.

Led by the scoutmaster, the boys dashed in that direction, filled whatever vessel they happened to be carrying, and then hurried back to the house. Here the water was dashed over the side of the building that seemed to be already scorching under the fierce heat of the blazing barn.

"Get us a ladder; that roof will be on fire if we don't throw water over it!" Paul shouted to the farmer, as he came in contact with the man.

"This way - there's a ladder here by the hen house!" was what he replied.

Several of the boys seized upon it, and before you could think twice they were rushing the ladder toward the side of the house. Paul climbed up, carrying with him a full bucket of water; and having dashed the contents of this in such a way as to wet a considerable portion of the shingle roof, he threw the bucket down to one of the boys below.

Another was quickly placed in his hands. Everybody was working like a beaver now, even the farmer's wife, carrying water from the creek, and getting it up to the boy on the ladder. It was pretty warm work, for the heat of the burning barn seemed terrific; but then boys can stand a good deal, especially when excited, and bent on accomplishing things; and Paul stuck it out, though he afterwards found several little holes had been burned in his outing shirt by flying sparks.

The barn, of course, was beyond saving, and all their energies must be expended on the house. By slow degrees the fire was burning itself out. Already Paul felt that the worst was past, and that if they could only keep this up for another ten minutes all would be well.

A couple of neighbors had come along by this time, to help as best they could. When a fire takes place in the country everybody is ready and willing to lend a hand at carrying out things, or fighting the flames in a primitive fashion; for neighbors have to depend more or less upon each other in case of necessity.

"I reckon the house ain't liable to go this time," Andy remarked, when Paul came down the ladder finally, trembling from his continued exertions, which had been considerable of a strain on the lad, wearied as he was with three days' tramping.

"That's a fact," remarked the farmer, who came hustling forward about this time, "and I owe you boys a heap for what you done this night. I guess now, only for you comin' to help, I'd a lost my house as well as my barn. As it is I've got a lot to be thankful for. Just put insurance on the barn, and the new crop of hay last week. I call that being pretty lucky for once."

He shook hands with each of the scouts, and asked after their names.

"I want to let your folks know what you done for us this night, boys," he said, "and p'raps you might accept some little present later on, just as a sort of remembrance, you know."

"How did the fire start, sir?" asked Paul.

"That's what bothers me a heap," replied the farmer.

"Then you don't know?" continued the scoutmaster, who felt a reasonable curiosity to learn what he could of the matter while on the spot.

"It's all a blank mystery to me, for a fact," continued the farmer, whose name the boys had learned was Mr. Rollins. "My barn and stable was all one, you see. My man has been away all day, and I had to look after the stock myself, but I finished just as dark set in, before supper, in fact, so there ain't been so much as a lighted lantern around here tonight."

"Perhaps, when you lighted your pipe you may have thrown the match away, and it fell in the hay?" suggested Paul.

"If it had, the fire'd started long ago; fact is, I'd a seen it right away. And to settle that right in the start let me say I don't smoke at all, and didn't have any occasion to strike a single match while out here."

Of course this statement of the farmer seemed to settle all idea of his having been in any way responsible for the burning of the barn.

"It looks like a big black mystery, all right," declared Fritz, who always liked to come upon some knotty problem that needed solving.

"Have you any idea that the fire could have been the work of tramps?" Paul went on to ask.

"We are never troubled that way up here," replied the farmer. "You see, it's away from the railroad, and hoboes generally follow the ties when they tramp across country."

"That makes it all the more queer how the fire could have started," Paul went on to remark, thoughtfully.

"Couldn't a been one of the cows taken to smoking, I suppose?" ventured Seth, in a humorous vein.

"One thing sure," continued the farmer, a little uneasily, "that fire must have been caused by what they call spontaneous combustion; or else somebody set it on purpose."

"Do you know of anybody who would do such a terrible thing; that is, have you any enemy that you know of, sir?" questioned Paul.

"None that I would ever suspect of such a mean thing as that," was the farmer's ready reply. "We're human around here, you know, and may have our little differences now and then, but they ain't none of 'em serious enough to tempt a man to burn a neighbor's barn. No, that's a dead sure thing."

"Well, I'm glad to hear it," the scoutmaster went on. "And I don't suppose now, you've missed any valuables, have you, sir?"

The farmer turned a shade whiter, and Paul could see that a shiver went through his frame.

"Gosh! I hadn't thought about that. Wait here a minute, will you, please?"

With that he dashed into the house, as though a sudden terrible suspicion had assailed him. The six scouts stood there awaiting his return. Mrs. Rollins was talking with the neighbors, as they watched the last of the barn disappearing in a bed of red cinders.

Hardly had a full minute passed before the boys saw the farmer come leaping out of the building again. No need for any one to ask a question, because his whole appearance told the story of new excitement and mystery. If ever a man looked worried and nearly heart broken the farmer did then.

"It's sure enough gone, every cent of it!" he groaned, as he reached the scouts.

"Your money, I suppose you mean?" Paul asked, sympathetically; while Fritz and Seth pricked up their ears eagerly at the prospect of another chapter being added to the little excitement of the evening.

"Yes, three thousand dollars that was to pay off my mortgage next week. I had it hid away where I thought no thief could even find it; but the little tin box, and everything has been carried off. And now I know why the barn was fired - so as to keep the missus and me out there, while the rascal made a sneak into the house, and laid hands on my savings. All gone, and the mortgage due next week!"

CHAPTER VI

THE HOME-COMING OF JO DAVIES

"Whew! that's tough!" observed Seth.

One or two of the other scouts whistled, to indicate the strained condition of their nerves; and all of them pressed up a little closer, so as not to lose a single word of what was passing.

"But if as you say, sir, that you had this money securely hidden, it doesn't seem possible that an ordinary tramp would know the place where you kept it, so that he could dodge right into the house, and in a minute be off with it; isn't that so?"

Paul was the greatest hand you ever heard of to dip deeply into a thing. Where most other boys of his age would be satisfied to simply listen, and wonder, he always persisted in asking questions, in order to get at the facts. And he was not born in Missouri either, as Seth often laughingly declared.

The farmer looked at him. There was a frown beginning to gather on his forehead as though sudden and serious doubts had commenced to take a grip on his mind.

"If he took my money I'll have the law on him, as sure as my name is Sile Rollins," Paul heard him mutter, half to himself.

"Then you've thought of some one who might have known that you had three thousand dollars under your roof, is that it, sir?" he asked.

"Y-yes, but it's hard to suspect Jo, when I've done so much for him these years he's been with me," admitted the owner of the farm; though at the same time his face took on a hard expression, and he ground his teeth together furiously, while he went on to say, "but if so be he has robbed me, I ain't called upon to have any mercy on him, just because his old mother once nursed my wife, and I guess saved her life. Jo has got to hand my money back, or take the consequences."

"Is Jo your hired man?" Paul asked.

The farmer nodded his head moodily; he was evidently a prey to mingled feelings, and close upon the border of a dazed condition. These calamities following so swiftly upon each other's heels had taken his breath away. But presently he would recover, and be eager to do something.

"You said just a bit ago that he was away today, and that you had to do the chores this evening, looking after the stock, and such things; wasn't that it, sir?" continued the scoutmaster.

"He asked to have this afternoon off; wouldn't say why he wanted to get away, either. And by ginger! now that I think of it, Jo did look kind of excited when he was asking me for leave. I can see why that should be so. He was figuring on this nasty little game right then and there. He wanted to be able to prove an *alibi* in case he was ever accused. And this evening he must have put a match to the hay in the barn, and then watched his chance to creep into the house when both of us was busy trying to save the stock. Oh! it makes my blood boil just to think of it. And I never would have believed Jo Davies could have been so cold blooded as to take the chances of burnin' the animals he seemed to be so fond of."

"Did he stay here over night with you?" Paul asked.

"Not as a rule, Jo didn't. You see, he's got an old mother, and

Archibald Lee Fletcher

they live in a little cottage about a mile away from here toward town. So Jo, he always made it a point to sleep there. I had no fault to find, because he was on hand bright and early every morning. But this will kill his old mother; however could he do it? Chances are, he fell in with some racing men when we had the county fair, and has got to gambling. But I'll be ruined if I don't get that money back again."

"Could we help you in any way, Mr. Rollins? You know, Boy Scouts are always bound to be of assistance whenever they find a chance. We're on a great hike just now, and a little leg weary; but if we can stand by you further, please let us know. How about that, boys?" and Paul turned toward his chums as he spoke.

"That's the ticket, Paul!" replied Andy, promptly.

"Our sentiments, every time," said Seth.

And the others gave vigorous nods, to indicate that they were all of the same mind; which unanimity of opinion must have been a great satisfaction to the leader.

"Then let's go right away, boys!" remarked the farmer, eagerly. "P'raps now we might come up with Jo on the way, and ketch him with the goods on. If he'll only give me back my money I'll agree not to prosecute, on account of his poor old mother, if nothing else. But I'm as bad off as a beggar if I lose all that hard earned cash."

Without saying anything to Mrs. Rollins or the neighbors, they hurried away, the boys keeping in a cluster around the farmer. If any of the scouts began to feel twinges in the muscles of their legs, already hard pushed, they valiantly fought against betraying the weakness. Besides, the excitement acted as a tonic upon them, and seemed to lend them additional powers of endurance, just as it does in foot races where the strain is terrific.

"It looks bad for Jo Davies, I should think, Paul," Andy managed to say, as they pushed resolutely along.

"Well, he is the one fellow who may have known about the money," admitted the scout master, "and if the temptation ever came to him, he could easily watch his employer, and learn where he hid the cash. How about that, Mr. Rollins?"

The farmer had heard what was being said, and immediately replied:

"If Jo was bent on robbery, p'raps he could have watched me some time, and seen where I hid that little tin box away in the attic. I used to go there once a week to add some money to the savings that I'd foolishly drawn out of bank long before I needed 'em, just to see how it felt to be rich for a little while."

"When was the last time you went up there to look at it?" Paul asked.

"Let me see, when Web Sterry paid me for the heifer I sold him I put the money away; and that was just ten days back."

"And it was all there then, you say?" questioned Paul.

"Surely," replied the farmer.

"Was Jo working near the house then, can you remember, sir?"

Mr. Rollins appeared to reflect.

"When was the day we did some carpenter work on that extension - as sure as anything it was the day Webb paid me! Yes, I remember, now, that Jo came around from his work on the plane, and told me Webb was there."

The farmer's excitement was increasing. Things, under the clever questioning of the young scoutmaster, seemed to be fitting in with each other, just as a carpenter dovetails the ends of a box together.

"It looks as though Jo might have spied on you when you went up to the attic to put that new money away with the rest. If he suspected that you were keeping a large sum in the house that's what he would most likely do when he knew you had just taken in some more cash. Now, I don't know Jo Davies, and I don't like to accuse him of such a terrible crime; but circumstantial evidence all points in his direction, Mr. Rollins."

Paul measured his words. He never liked to think ill of any one; but really in this case it seemed as though there could be hardly any doubt at all; Jo Davies must be the guilty party.

"Are we gettin' near where Jo lives?" asked Jotham, trying to speak lightly, although there was a plain vein of anxiety in his voice; for when a fellow has covered nearly thirty miles since sun-up, every rod counts after that; and following each little rest the muscles seem to stiffen wonderfully.

"More'n two-thirds the way there," replied the farmer. "We'll see a light, like as not, when we get around this turn in the woods road. That'll come from the little cabin where he lives with his old mother. Oh! but I'm sorry for Mrs. Davies; and the boy, he always seemed to think so much of his maw, too. You never can tell, once these fast fliers get to running with racing men. But I only hope I get my own back again. That's the main thing with me just now, you know. And if Jo, he seems sorry, I might try and forget what he's done. It all depends on how things turn out. See, just as I told you, there's the light ahead."

All of them saw it; and as they continued to walk hastily forward through the darkness Paul was thinking how human Mr. Rollins was, after all; for it was only natural that his first thought should be in connection with the safe recovery of his hard earned money.

They rapidly drew near the cottage, and all of the boys were beginning to wonder what was fated to happen next on the programme. Doubtless they were some of them fairly quivering with eagerness, and hoping that the thief might be caught examining the stolen cash box.

"Hush! there's somebody coming along over there; stand still, everybody!" Paul gave warning, suddenly, and the whole party remained motionless, watching a lighted lantern that was moving rapidly toward the cottage from the opposite direction, being evidently carried by an approaching man.

It continued to advance straight toward the cottage. Then the unknown opened the door, and went in.

"That was Jo," muttered Mr. Rollins, "I seen his face plain as anything; but why would he be coming from the direction of town, instead of my place?"

"Oh! that might be only a clever little trick, sir," Seth made haste to say, as though to indicate in this way that scouts were able to see back of all such sly dodges.

"Say, he sure had something under his arm," broke in Jotham just then.

"Yes, I saw that, too," added Paul. "It was a small package, not much larger than a cigar box, I should say, and wrapped up in brown paper."

"P'raps my tin cash box?" suggested Mr. Rollins, in trembling tones.

"It might be, though I hardly think any one smart enough to play such a game as setting fire to a barn in order to draw all attention away from the house he wanted to rob, would be silly enough to carry home a tin box that would convict him, if ever it was found there."

Paul made this remark. They had once more started to

advance, though by no means as rapidly as before. The fact that Jo Davies had arrived just before them, and not only carrying a lighted lantern, but with a suspicious packet under his arm, seemed to necessitate a change of pace, as well as a new line of action.

"Let's sneak up to the window, and peek in?" suggested Fritz, and somehow the idea appealed to the others, for without any argument they proceeded to carry out the plan of campaign.

It promised to be easy work. The shade seemed to be all the way up, as though the old lady who lived in the humble cottage had left a light near the window purposely in order to cheer her boy when he turned the bend below, and came in sight of home.

As noiselessly as possible, therefore, the six scouts, accompanied by the farmer, crept toward this window. The sill was not over four feet from the ground, and could be easily reached; indeed, in order not to expose themselves, they were compelled to stoop rather low when approaching the spot.

Some sort of flower garden lay under the window. Paul remembered stepping upon unseen plants, and somehow felt a pang of regret at thus injuring what had probably taken much of the old lady's time and attention to nurse along to the flowering stage. But this was an occasion when all minor scruples must be laid aside. When a man has been basely robbed, and by an employee in whom he has put the utmost confidence, one cannot stand on ceremony, even if pet flower-beds are rudely demolished. And if the farmer's suspicions turned out to be real facts, Jo Davies' old mother was apt to presently have worries besides which the breaking of her flowers would not be a circumstance.

Now they had reached a point where, by raising their heads, they could peep into the room where the lamp gave such illumination.

As scouts the boys had long ago learned to be cautious in whatever they attempted; and hence they did not immediately thrust their heads upward, at the risk of attracting the attention of whoever might be within the room. On the contrary each fellow slowly and carefully raised himself, inch by inch, until his eyes, having passed the lower sill he could see, first the low ceiling, then the upper part of the opposite wall, and last of all the occupants themselves.

They were two in number, one an old woman with a sweet face and snow-white hair; the other a tall, boyish-looking chap, undoubtedly the Jo who had been farmhand to Mr. Rollins, and was now under the dreadful ban of suspicion.

When Paul first caught sight of these two they were bending over the table, on which something evidently lay that had been holding their attention. Jo was talking excitedly. Every minute he would pause in whatever he was saying, to throw his arms around the little old lady, who in turn would clasp her arms about his neck; and in this way they seemed to be exchanging mutual congratulations. But when they moved aside while thus embracing, Paul felt a cold chill run up and down his spine because *there upon the table were several piles of bank bills*!

Archibald Lee Fletcher

CHAPTER VII

INNOCENT OR GUILTY?

Paul could feel the farmer trembling as he happened to come in contact with his person; and from this he guessed that Mr. Rollins had also discovered the pile of money on the table.

Was Jo Davies, then, such a silly fellow as this? It did not seem possible that anyone not a fool would rob his employer, and immediately hurry home, to throw the stolen money before his dear old mother, with some wonderful story of how he had found it on the road, perhaps, or had it given to him by a millionaire whose horse he stopped on the highway, when it was running away with a lady in the vehicle.

And somehow, from the few little glimpses Paul had caught of the young fellow's face he rather liked Jo Davies. If, as seemed very likely, the young man had been tempted to steal this money, it would cause Paul a feeling of regret, even though he had not known there was such a being as Jo Davies in the world half an hour before.

"Whoo! see the long green!" he heard Seth whisper. "Reckon he's gone and done it, worse luck!" and from the words and the manner of his saying them, Paul guessed that the speaker must have taken a fancy to Jo, as well as himself.

The window happened to be shut, and so this whisper attracted no attention on the part of those within the cottage.

Indeed, they were so given over to excitement themselves that they were hardly apt to notice anything out of the common.

Paul could feel the farmer beginning to slip down, and it was easy to understand that the sight of all that money made him want to rush inside, to claim it, before the bold thief had a chance to hide his plunder somewhere.

And this was the only possible thing that should be done. While Mr. Rollins in the kindness of his heart might wish to spare the dear old lady all he could, he dared not take any chances of losing sight of his property.

"Come on, boys!"

That was quite enough, for when the other scouts heard Paul say these three simple words they knew that there was going to be something doing. And quickly did they proceed to fall in behind their leader and the farmer.

Under ordinary conditions, perhaps, it might have occurred to the patrol leader to throw some sort of guard around the cabin, so as to prevent the escape of the desperate thief. He did not think of doing such a thing now, for various reasons.

In the first place, one of the scouts could hardly hope to cope with such a husky young fellow as the farmhand, if once he wanted to break through the line.

Then again, it hardly seemed likely that Jo Davies would attempt to flee, when his old mother was there to witness his confusion; in fact, the chances appeared to be that he would brazen it out, and try to claim that the money belonged to him. The door was close at hand, so that it took only part of a minute for the eager farmer to reach the means of ingress.

He did not hesitate a second, after having set eyes on all that alluring pile of bank notes on the table, under the glow of the lamp.

And when he suddenly opened the door, to burst into the room, Paul and the other scouts were close upon his heels, every fellow anxious to see what was about to happen.

Of course the noise caused by their entrance in such a mass, was heard by those in the room. Jo Davies sprang to his feet, and assumed an attitude of defiance, one arm extended, as though to defend the little fortune that lay there exposed so recklessly upon the table.

Possibly this was the very first time in all his life that he had experienced such a sensation as fear of robbery. When a man has never possessed anything worth stealing, he can hardly know what the feeling is. So it must have been sheer instinct that caused Jo to thus stand on guard, ready apparently to fight, in order to protect his property, however recently it may have come into his possession.

No wonder that he felt this sudden alarm, to have the door of his home rudely thrown open, and a horde of fellows fairly tumbling over each other, in their eagerness to enter.

Then, the look of alarm seemed to pass away from the face of the young fellow; as though he had recognized his employer. Paul wondered whether this was real or cleverly assumed. He saw Jo actually smile, and advancing a step, half hold out his hand toward Mr. Rollins.

But the farmer was looking very stern just then. He either did not see the extended hand, or else meant to ignore it purposely, for he certainly made no move toward taking it.

"I've got back, Mr. Rollins," Jo said, his voice rather shaky, either from excitement, or some other reason; and he stared hard at Paul and the other khaki-garbed scouts, as though puzzled to account for their being there.

"So I see," replied the farmer, grimly.

"I hope you didn't hev too much trouble with the stock, Mr. Rollins," Jo went on to say, in a half hesitating sort of way.

"Well, if I did, they are all safe and sound; perhaps you'd like to know that now," the farmer went on to remark, a little bitterly.

Jo looked at him queerly.

"He either doesn't understand what that means, or else is trying to seem ignorant," was what Paul thought, seeing this expression of wonderment.

"I'm glad to hear that, sure I am, Mr. Rollins," the other remarked, slowly, "an' seein' as how you're dropped in on us unexpected like, p'raps I ought to tell you what I meant to say in the mornin.'"

"What's that?" demanded Mr. Rollins, unconsciously edging a little closer to the table where that tempting display of greenbacks could be seen; just as though he began to fear that it might suddenly take wings and fly away before he could put in a claim for his property.

"I've come in for a little windfall, sir," began Jo, proudly it appeared.

"Looks like you had," grumbled the farmer, as he flashed his eyes again toward the display so near at hand.

"And if so be you're of the same mind about that Thatcher farm, p'raps we might come to terms about the same, sir. I guess you'd just as lief sell it to *me* as anybody else, wouldn't you, Mr. Rollins?"

"You seem to have a lot of money all of a sudden, Jo?" suggested the farmer, in a hoarse tone, so that he had to clear his throat twice while speaking.

"Yes, sir, that's so," declared the young farm hand, eagerly. "I never dreamed of such grand good fortune as an old aunt of mine dying up in Indianapolis, and leaving me all she had in bank. That's why I asked to get off this afternoon, Mr. Rollins, so I could run over, and get what was comin' to me."

The farmer was grinding his teeth a little; but so long as he believed he saw all his stolen hoard before him, within reach of his hand, he seemed able to control himself; he even waxed a trifle sarcastic, Paul thought, when, looking straight at his hired man, he went on to say:

"Perhaps now, Jo, I might give a pretty good guess about the size of this wonderful fortune you've come into so sudden-like. How would three thousand sound to you, Jo? Is that about the figure now, tell me?"

Jo turned a wondering face toward his old mother.

"Well, did you ever hear the beat of that, maw?" he cried, "Mr. Rollins has just guessed the size of my pile to a dollar, because it was just three thousand old Aunt Libby left me - a few dollars over p'raps. However did you know it, sir?" and he once more faced the sneering farmer.

"I'll tell you, Jo," continued Mr. Rollins, coldly, "I happen to have just had three thousand dollars in bills stolen from my house this very night, by some rascal who first of all set fire to my stable and barn, so that the missus and me'd be so taken up with saving our pet stock we'd leave the farmhouse unguarded. Yes, and there *was* a few dollars more'n three thousand dollars, Jo. Queer coincidence I'd call it now,
wouldn't you?"

Jo turned deathly white, and stared at his employer. His eyes were round with real, or assumed horror. If he was "putting on," as Seth would term it, then this farm hand must be a pretty clever actor for a crude country bumpkin, Paul thought.

"Oh! Jo, my boy, my boy, what does he mean by saying that?"

The little old lady had arisen from her chair, though she trembled so that she seemed in danger of falling; but Paul unconsciously moved a pace closer, ready to catch her in his arms if she swooned. But Jo, quick as a flash, hearing her voice, whirled around, and threw a protecting arm about her.

"It's all right, maw; don't you go and be afraid. I ain't done nawthing you need to be fearful about. This money's mine! Set down again, deary. Don't you worrit about Jo. He ain't agoin' to make your dear old heart bleed, sure he ain't."

And somehow, when Paul saw the tender way in which the rough farm boy forced the little old lady back into her chair, and caught the positive tone in which he gave her this assurance, he seemed almost ready to believe Jo *must* be innocent; although when he glanced at the money his heart misgave him again.

"Now, Mr. Rollins, please tell me what it all means?" asked Jo, turning and facing his employer again, with a bold, self-confident manner that must have astonished the farmer not a little. "I just come up from town as fast as I could hurry, because, you see, I knew I was bringin' the greatest of news to maw here. I did see a sorter light in the sky when I was leavin' town, and thinks I to myself, that old swamp back of the ten acre patch must be burnin' again; but I never dreamed it was the stable and hay barn, sure I didn't sir."

The farmer hardly seemed to know what to say to this, he was so taken aback by the utter absence of guilt in the face and manner of Jo.

Before he could frame any sort of reply the young fellow had spoken again.

"You said as how you'd got all the stock out safe, didn't you, Mr. Rollins? I'd just hate to think of Polly and Sue and the hosses bein' burned up. Whatever d'ye think could a set the fire agoin'? Mebbe that last hay we put in wa'n't as well cured as it might a been, an' it's been heatin' right along. I meant to look into it more'n once, but somethin' always came along an' I plumb forgot it."

Mr. Rollins looked at him, and frowned. He did not know how to answer such a lead as this. He was growing impatient, almost angry again.

"Give me my money, Jo, and let me be going; I can't breathe proper in here, you've upset me so bad," he said, holding out his hand with an imperative gesture.

"But I ain't got no money of yours, Mr. Rollins," expostulated the other, stubbornly. "I'm awful sorry if you've gone and lost your roll, and I'd do most anything to help you find it again; but that money belongs to me, and I don't mean to turn it over to nobody. It's goin' to buy a home for me and maw, understand that, sir - your little Thatcher place, if so be you'll come to terms; but some other if you won't. That's plain, sir, ain't it?"

"What, do you have the nerve to stick to that silly story, after admitting that this wonderfully gotten fortune of yours tallies to the dollar with what has been taken from my house?" demanded Mr. Rollins, acting as though half tempted to immediately pounce upon the treasure, and take possession, depending on Paul and his scouts to back him up if Jo showed fight.

"I sure do; and I know what I know, Mr. Rollins!" declared the farmhand, with flashing eyes, as he pushed between the table and the irate farmer; while his little mother wrung her clasped hands, and moaned pitifully to see the strange thing that was happening there under her own roof.

It looked for a moment as though there might be some sort of a rumpus; and Seth even began to clench his hands as if ready to take a prominent part in the same; but as had happened more than a few times before when the storm clouds gathered over the scouts, Paul's wise counsel intervened to prevent actual hostilities.

"Wait a minute, Mr. Rollins," he called out. "This thing ought to be easily settled, one way or another. You understand that queer things may happen sometimes, and there is a chance that two sums of money may be almost exactly alike. Now, if Jo here has inherited a nice little fortune, he ought to be able to prove that to us by showing letters, or some sort of documents. How about that, Jo?"

To the surprise, and pleasure as well, of the scoutmaster, Jo's face immediately expanded into a wide grin, and he nodded his head eagerly.

"Say, maw, what did you do with that letter we had from the law firm over in Indianapolis, tellin' me to come and claim my property, and to bring along something to prove that I was the said Jo Albion Davies mentioned in Aunt Selina's last will and testament? In the drawer, you mean? All right, I'll get it; and let these gentlemen read the same. And there's Squire McGregor as went up with me to identify me to the lawyers, he'll tell you he saw me get this money from the bank, just before they closed this arternoon. There she is; now read her out loud, young feller."

CHAPTER VIII

"WELL, OF ALL THINGS!"

"All right; I'll be only too glad to do the same," said Paul, as he accepted what appeared to be a well thumbed letter from Jo.

One glance he gave at the same, and then a load seemed to have been lifted somehow from his boyish heart; because, after he had seen how Jo Davies loved that dear little white-haired mother, he would have felt it keenly did the circumstances make it appear that the young farmhand were guilty of robbing the man who trusted him so fully.

So Paul read out the letter. There is no need of giving it here, because it was rather long, and written in a very legal-like way, each sentence being enveloped in a ponderous atmosphere.

But it was upon the letter-head of a big law firm in Indianapolis, and in so many words informed the said Jo Albion Davies that his respected aunt, Selina Lee Davies, had passed out of this life, leaving him her sole heir; and that if he were interested, it would be to his advantage to come to the city as speedily as possible, to claim the little sum that was waiting for him in bank; and to be sure and bring some one along with him who would be able to vouch for his being the party in question.

Luckily Jo had taken Squire McGregor along, who happened to know one of the members of the big law firm; for otherwise the heir might have had some trouble in proving his identity, since he had forgotten to carry even the letter in his pocket, it seemed.

But of course after that Mr. Rollins could not say a word about claiming the tempting display of greenbacks that lay exposed upon the table. Jo was already engaged in tenderly gathering them up, as though meaning to secrete his little fortune either on his person, or somewhere else.

"Looks like I'm clean busted, don't it?" the farmer said, with a sigh, turning toward Paul, upon whom he had somehow come to rely in the strangest way possible.

"It does seem as though your money has gone in a queer way, sir," replied the young scoutmaster, "but honestly now, I find it hard to believe that a common hobo would be able to find it so quick, if you had it hidden away up in a corner of the garret, and hadn't been there for ten days."

Jo stopped gathering his fortune together; he had snapped several heavy rubber bands around it, evidently supplied at the city bank when he drew the money.

"I wonder, now, could that have anything to do with it," they heard him mutter, as he looked curiously at the farmer.

The words were heard by Mr. Rollins, who, ready to grasp at a floating straw, in his extremity, even as might a drowning man, quickly observed:

"What do you mean by saying that, Jo? I hope you can give me some sort of hint that will help me find my money again; because I meant to pay off my mortgage with it, and will be hard pushed to make good, if it stays lost."

"I'll tell you, sir," said Jo, readily. "It was just about a week ago that I'd been to town, you remember, and getting home along about midnight I was worried about one of the hosses that had been actin' sick like. So I walked over here, not wantin' to wait till mornin'. Just when I was agoin' back I seen a light movin' around over at the house, and I stopped a minute to watch the same."

"Yes, go on; a week ago, you say?" the farmer remarked, as Jo paused to catch his breath again.

"On Thursday night it was, Mr. Rollins," the other went on. "Well, just then I saw the back door open, and somebody stepped out. I seen it was you, and about the queerest part of it all was that it looked to me as if you might be walkin' around in your pajamas! Do you remember comin' outdoors on that night for anything, sir?"

"I don't even remember walking around that way," replied Mr. Rollins, hastily, and looking as though he did not know whether Jo were trying to play some sort of joke on him, or not, "but go on and tell the rest. What did I do? Did you stop long enough to see?"

"Well," continued the farm hand, "I saw you go over to the old Dutch oven that hasn't been used this twenty years, and move around there a bit; but it wasn't none of my business, Mr. Rollins, and so I went along home. I guess any gentleman's got the right to go wanderin' around his own premises in the middle of the night, if he wants to, and nobody ain't got any right to complain because he don't make the trouble to put on his day clothes."

The farmer looked helplessly at Paul. Plainly his wits were in a stupor, and he could not make head or tail of what Jo was telling him.

"Can you get a pointer on to what it all means?" he asked, almost piteously.

Paul had conceived a wonderful idea that seemed to give great promise of solving the dark puzzle.

"You just as much as said that you could not remember having come out of your house that night; and that you never knew yourself to walk around out of doors in your pajamas; is that so, sir?" he asked.

"That's what I meant; and if I was put on the stand right now, I could lift my right hand, and take my solemn affidavit that I didn't do any such thing - unless by George! I was walking in my sleep!"

"That's just the point I'm trying to get at, Mr. Rollins," said Paul, quietly. "Jo, here, says he *saw* you as plain as anything, and yet you don't recollect doing it. See here, sir, can you ever remember walking in your sleep?"

"Why, not for a great many years," answered the farmer, somewhat confused, and yet with a new gleam of hope appearing in his expectant eyes.

"But you admit then that you *have* done such a thing?" pursued the scoutmaster.

"Yes, as a boy I did a heap of queer stunts when asleep. They had to lock my door for a time, and fasten my windows. Why, one night they found me sitting on top of the chimney, and had to wait till I took the notion to come down; because, if they woke me, it might mean a nasty tumble that would like as not break my neck. But I haven't done anything in that line for thirty years."

"Until one night a week ago, Mr. Rollins," continued Paul, convincingly, "when dreaming that your money was in danger, you got out of your bed, went up and took it from the garret where you had it hidden, walked downstairs, passed outside, and stowed it nicely away inside the big old Dutch oven. And chances are you'll find it right there this minute."

"Oh! do you really think so, my boy?" exclaimed the delighted farmer, "then I'm going off right away and find out. If you'll go with me I'll promise to hitch up, and carry the lot of you back to your camp, no matter where that may be."

"What say, shall we go, fellows?" asked the patrol leader, turning to the others.

There was not one dissenting voice. Every boy was just wild to ascertain how this strange mystery would turn out. And as it would be just about as long a walk to Alabama Camp as going to the farmer's place, they decided the matter without any argument.

"And you just bet I'm going along, after what I've heard about this thing," declared Jo Davies, "maw, you ain't afraid to stay alone a little while longer, be you? You c'n sit on this blessed windfall while I'm gone, but don't go to fingerin' the same, because walls often have eyes as well as ears, remember."

When the six scouts started off in company with Mr. Rollins, Jo Davies tagged along with them. In his own good fortune the farm hand was only hoping that the money which his employer had missed might be found in the old Dutch oven, just like this smart Boy Scout had suggested.

They covered the distance in short order. You would never have believed that those agile lads had been walking for nearly twelve hours that day, if you could see how they got over the ground, even with two of them limping.

It can be easily understood that there was more or less speculation among the scouts as they hurried along. Would the farmer find his missing wad snugly secreted in the old Dutch oven, as Paul so confidently suggested? And if such turned out to be the case, wouldn't it prove that the scoutmaster was a wonder at guessing things that were a blank puzzle to everybody else?

So they presently came again to the farm. The ashes were still glowing where the big barn had so recently stood. Here and there a cow or a horse could be seen, nosing around in the half light, picking at the grass in forbidden corners, and evidently about done with their recent fright.

Straight toward the back of the house the farmer led the way, and up to the old Dutch oven that had been built on to the foundation, for the baking of bread, and all family purposes, many years back; but which had fallen into disuse ever since the new coal range had been placed in the kitchen.

Everybody fairly held their breath as Mr. Rollins dropped down on his hands and knees, struck a match, and half disappeared within the huge receptacle. He came backing out almost immediately; and before his head and shoulders appeared in view Paul knew that he had made a glorious find, because they could hear him laughing almost hysterically.

"Just like you said, my boy, it was there!" he cried, holding up what proved to be the missing tin box that held his hoard. "And to think that I stole my own cash while I was asleep! I guess my wife'll have to tie my feet together every night after this, for a while; or perhaps I'll be running away with everything we've got. Say, Jo, I hope you ain't going to hold it against me that I suspected you'd been and had your morals corrupted by some of them horse jockeys you met at the county fair this summer? And about that Thatcher place, Jo, we'll easy make terms, because nobody ain't going to have it but you and your maw, hear that?"

"Well, of all things," exclaimed the delighted Seth.

Jo evidently did not hold the slightest ill feeling against his old friend and employer, for he only too gladly took the hand Mr. Rollins held out.

"Turns out just like the fairy story, with everybody happy; only we don't see the princess this time," said Seth, after the scouts had given three cheers for Jo, and then three more for Mr. Rollins.

"Oh!" remarked Jo, with a huge grin, "she's comin' along purty soon now; and my gettin' this windfall'll hurry up the weddin' a heap. Drop past the Thatcher farm along about Thanksgivin' time, boys, and I'll be glad to introduce you to her."

"Say, perhaps we will," Seth declared, with boyish enthusiasm, "because, you see, we all live at Beverly, which ain't more'n twenty miles away as the crow flies. How about it, fellows?"

"We'll come along with you, Seth, never fear. And now, the sooner we get over to camp the better, because some of us are feeling pretty well used up," Andy went on to admit with charming candor.

"All right, boys, just give me a minute to run indoors, and put this package away, and I'll be with you. It won't take long to hitch up, because we managed to save the harness and wagons, me and the missus."

True to his word Mr. Rollins was back in a very brief space of time, and catching the two horses he wanted, he attached them to a big wagon.

"Tumble in, boys," he called out, as he swung himself up on the driver's seat, after attaching the lighted lantern to the front, so that he could see the road as they went along.

The scouts waited for no second invitation, but speedily secured places in the body of the vehicle. As there was half a foot of straw in it, they found things so much to their liking that on the way, at least three of the boys went sound asleep, and had to be aroused when the camp was finally reached.

Eben and Noodles were poor sentinels, it seemed, for both were lying on the ground asleep, nor did they know when the other returned until told about it in the morning. But fortune had been kind to the "babes in the wood," as Seth called them in derision, for nothing had happened while the main body of the patrol chanced to be away on duty.

And so it was another little adventure had come along, with wonderful results, and the happiest of endings. Really, some of the boys were beginning to believe that the strangest of happenings were always lying in wait, as if desirous of ambushing the members of the Beaver Patrol. Why, they could even not start off on a hike, it seemed, without being drawn into a series of events, the like of which seldom if ever befell ordinary lads.

During the hours of darkness that followed all of them slept soundly, nor was there any alarm given to disturb them. And as nothing in the wide world brings such satisfaction and contentment as good sleep, when at dawn they awoke to find the last day of the great hike at hand, every fellow declared that he was feeling especially fit to make that concluding dash with a vim.

Breakfast was hastily eaten; indeed, their stock of provisions had by this time gotten to a low ebb, and would not allow of much variety; though they managed to scrape enough together to satisfy everybody but Fritz, who growled a little, and wanted to know however a scout could do his best when on short rations?

Then to the inspiring notes of Eben's silver-plated bugle the boys of the Beaver Patrol left Alabama Camp, and started on the last lap for their home goal.

Archibald Lee Fletcher

CHAPTER IX

THE RUNAWAY BALLOON

"Hey! look at all the crows flying over, would you?"

Seth called this out as he pointed upwards, and the rest of the patrol naturally turned their heads in order to gape.

"Whew! did you ever see such a flock of the old caw-caws?" burst out Eben.

"Give 'em a toot from your bugle, and see what they think?" suggested Jotham.

"For goodness sake, be careful," broke in Fritz, "because they might be so knocked in a heap at Eben's fine playing, they'd take a tumble, and nearly smother the lot of us. We'd think it was raining crow, all right."

"Are they good to eat?" demanded Babe, who was pretty green as yet to a great many things connected with outdoor life, "because, if we have time to stop at noon to cook a meal, we might -"

He was interrupted by a shout from several of the other and wiser scouts.

"Say, hold on there, Babe, we haven't got that near being starved as to want to eat crow," declared Andy.

"Can they be eaten at all, Paul?" persisted Babe, as usual turning to the scoutmaster for information; "seems to me I've heard something like that."

"Yes, and people who have tried say they're not near as bad a dish as the papers always make out," Paul replied. "I don't see myself why they should be, when most of the time they live on the farmer's corn."

"But can you tell where that bunch is coming from, and where bound?" continued Babe. "They all come out of that same place, and keep chattering as they soar on the wind, which must be some high up there."

"Well, I've heard it said that there's a big crow rookery somewhere back in the gloomy old Black Water Swamps; but I never met anybody that had ever set eyes on the same. Every day, winter and summer, that big flock comes out, and scatters to a lot of feeding grounds; some going down the river, where they pick up food that's been cast ashore; others bound for a meal in the corn fields."

"And they come back again in the night to roost there; is that it, Paul?"

"Yes, I guess if we stood right here half an hour before dark we'd see squads of the noisy things heading over yonder from all sorts of quarters. D'ye know, I've sometimes had a notion I'd like to explore the heart of that queer old swamp," and the young patrol leader cast a thoughtful glance toward the quarter from whence that seemingly endless stream of crows flowed continually.

"Hurrah! that's the ticket!" exclaimed Seth. "I've heard a heap about that same spooky old place myself. They say nobody ever has been able to get to the heart of it. And I heard one man, who traps quite a lot of muskrats every winter, tell how he got lost in a part of the swamp once, and spent a couple of pretty tough days and nights wandering around, before he found his way out again. He said it'd take a heap to tempt him to try and poke into the awful center of Black Water Swamps."

"But what's that to us, fellers?" ejaculated Fritz. "The boys of the Beaver Patrol ain't the kind to get scared at such a little thing as a swamp. Just because it's a tough proposition ought to make us want to take up the game, and win out. We fairly eat hard jobs! And looking back we have a right to feel a little proud of the record we've made, eh, fellers?"

Of course every scout stood up a little straighter at these words, and smiled with the consciousness that they had, as Fritz so aptly put it, a right to feel satisfied with certain things that had happened in the past, and from which they had emerged acknowledged victors.

"Just put a pin in that, to remember it, Paul, won't you?" said Andy.

"Why, sure I will, since a lot of you seem to think it worth while," replied the obliging scoutmaster, with a smile, "and if we haven't anything ahead that seems to be more worth while, we might turn out here later on, prepared to survey a trail right through the swamp. I admit that I'm curious myself to see what lies hidden away in a place where, up to now, no man has ever set a foot."

"Hurrah for the young explorers!" cried Eben, who seemed strangely thrilled at the tempting prospect.

They say the boy is father to the man; and among a bunch of six or eight lads it is almost a certainty that you will find one or two who fairly yearn to grow up, and be second Livingstones, or Stanleys, or Dr. Kanes. Eben had read many books concerning the amazing doings of these pathfinders of civilisation, and doubtless even dreamed his boyish dreams that some fine day he too might make the name of Newcomb famous on the pages of history by discovering some hitherto unknown tribe of black dwarfs; or charting out a land that had always been unexplored territory.

They looked back many times at the stream of flying crows that continued to issue from that one point beyond the thick woods. And somehow the very prospect of later on trying to accomplish a task that had until then defied all who had attempted it, gave the scouts a pleasing thrill of anticipation. For such is boy nature.

Strange how things often come about.

Just at that moment not one of the scouts even dreamed of what was in store for them. How many times the curtain obscures our sight, even when we are on the very threshold of discovery!

They tramped along sturdily, until they had covered perhaps two miles since departing from the place where the third night had been spent, and which would go down in the record of the big hike as Camp Alabama.

A couple of the scouts limped perceptibly, but even they declared that as they went on the "kinks" were getting out of their legs, and presently all would be well.

The sun shone from a fair sky, though now and then a cloud would pass over his smiling face; but as the day promised to be rather hot none of them were sorry for this.

"Hope it don't bring a storm along, though," remarked Babe, when the matter was under discussion.

"Well, it's got to be some storm to keep the boys of the Beaver Patrol from finishing their hike on time," declared Seth, grimly.

"That's so, Seth, you never spoke truer words," added Fritz. "I reckon, now, half of Beverly will turn out on the green this after noon to see the conquering heroes come home. There's been the biggest crowds around that jeweler's window all week, staring at that handsome cup, and wishing they would have a chance to help win it."

"And we'd hate the worst kind to disappoint our friends and folks, wouldn't we, fellers?" Eben remarked.

Somehow both limpers forgot to give way to their weakness, and from that minute on the very thought of the great crowd that would send up a tremendous cheer when the boys in khaki came in sight, was enough to make them walk as though they did not know such a thing as getting tired.

"Look!" cried Fritz, a couple of minutes afterwards, "oh! my stars! what's that big thing rising up behind the tops of the trees over there?"

"Somebody's barn is blowing away, I guess!" exclaimed Eben, in tones that shook with sudden alarm. "Mebbe's it's a cyclone acomin', boys. Paul, what had we ought to do? It ain't safe to be under trees at such a time, I've heard!"

"Cyclone, your granny!" jeered Seth Carpenter, who had very sharp eyes, and was less apt to get "rattled" at the prospect of sudden danger, than the bugler of Beverly Troop, "why, as sure as you live, I believe it's a balloon, Paul!"

"What! a real and true balloon?" almost shrieked Eben, somewhat relieved at the improved prospect.

"You're right, Seth," declared the scoutmaster, "it *is* a balloon, and it looks to me right now as though there's been trouble for the aeronaut. That gas-bag has a tough look to me, just as if it had lost about half of the stuff that keeps it floating! See how it wabbles, will you, fellows, and how low down over the trees it hangs. There, it just grazed that bunch of oaks on the little rise. The next time it'll get caught, and be ripped to pieces!"

"Paul, do you think that can be a man hanging there?" cried

Seth. "Sometimes it looks to me like it was; and then again the balloon tilts over so much I just can't be sure."

"We'll know soon enough," remarked the patrol leader, quietly, "because, as you can see, the runaway balloon is heading this way, full tilt. I wouldn't be surprised if it passed right over our heads."

"Say, perhaps we might grab hold of some trailing rope, and bring the old thing down?" suggested Fritz, looking hastily around him while speaking, as if desirous of being prepared, as a true scout should always make it a point to be, and have his tree picked out, about which he would hastily wind a rope, should he be fortunate enough to get hold of such.

"Whew! I wouldn't want to be in that feller's shoes," observed Eben, as they all stood there in the road, watching the rapidly approaching balloon.

"Solid ground for me, every time, except when I'm in swimming, or skimming along over the ice in winter!" Andy interjected, without once removing his eager eyes from the object that had so suddenly caught their attention.

It was a sight calculated to hold the attention of any one, with that badly battered balloon sweeping swiftly along on the wind, and approaching so rapidly.

All of them could see that there was a man clinging to the ropes that marked the place where the customary basket should have been; evidently this latter must have been torn away during a collision with the rocks or trees on the top of a ridge with which the ungovernable gas-bag had previously been in contact; and it was a marvel how the aeronaut had been able to cling there.

"Will it land near here, d'ye think, Paul?" asked Jotham, round-eyed with wonder, and feeling very sorry for the wretched traveler of the upper air currents, who seemed to be in deadly peril of his life.

"I hardly think so," replied the scoutmaster, rapidly measuring distances with his ready eye, and calculating upon the drop of the half collapsed balloon.

"But see where the bally old thing's heading, will you?" cried Seth, "straight at the place where them crows came out of. Say, wouldn't it be awful tough now, if it dropped right down in the heart of Black Water Swamps, where up to now never a human being has set foot, unless some Indian did long ago, when the Shawnees and Sacs and Pottawattomies and all that crowd rampaged through this region flat-footed."

The scouts stood there, and watched with tense nerves as the drifting balloon drew rapidly closer.

Now they could plainly see the man. He had secured himself in some way among the broken ropes that had doubtless held the basket in place. Yes, and he must have discovered the presence of the little khaki-clad band of boys on the road, for surely he was waving his hand to them wildly now.

Perhaps he understood that it was a safe thing to appeal to any boy who wore that well known suit; because every one has learned by this time that when a lad takes upon himself the duties and obligations of scoutcraft, he solemnly promises to always help a fellow in distress, when the opportunity comes along; and with most scouts the habit has become so strong that they always keep both eyes open, looking for just such openings.

Closer and closer came the wrecked air monster.

Just as one of the boys had said, it seemed about to pass very nearly overhead; and as the man would not be more than sixty or seventy feet above them, possibly he might be able to shout out a message.

"Keep still! He's calling something down to us!" cried Seth, when several of the others had started to chatter at a lively rate.

Now the balloon was whipping past, going at a pretty good clip. Apparently, then, it did not mean to get quite low enough to let them clutch any trailing rope, and endeavor to effect the rescue of the aeronaut. Fritz did make an upward leap, and try to lay hold of the only rope that came anywhere near them; but missed it by more than a foot.

"Accident - badly wrenched leg - follow up, and bring help - Anderson, from St. Louis - balloon *Great Republic* - report me as down - will drop in few minutes!"

They caught every word, although the man's voice seemed husky, and weak, as if he might have been long exposed and suffering. And as they stood and watched the balloon drift steadily away, lowering all the time, every one of those eight scouts felt moved by a great feeling of pity for the valiant man who had risked his life and was now in such a desperate situation.

"There she goes down, fellers!" cried Eben, excitedly.

"And what d'ye know, the bally old balloon has taken a crazy notion to drop right in the worst part of the Black Water Swamps, where we were just saying nobody had ever been before!"

Archibald Lee Fletcher

CHAPTER X

DUTY ABOVE ALL THINGS

"Gee! whiz! that's tough!"

Fritz gave vent to his overwrought feelings after this boyish fashion; and his words doubtless echoed the thought that was in the mind of every fellow in that little bunch of staring scouts.

True enough, the badly damaged balloon had taken a sudden dip downward, as though unable to longer remain afloat, with such a scanty supply of gas aboard; and as Seth said, it certainly looked as though it had chosen the very worst place possible to drop - about in the heart of the swamp.

"Now, why couldn't the old thing have dipped low enough right here for us to grab that trailing rope?" demanded Jotham, dejectedly; for he immediately began to feel that all manner of terrible things were in store for the aeronaut, if, as seemed likely, he would be marooned in the unknown morass, with no means of finding his way out, and an injured leg in the bargain to contend with.

"Hope he didn't come down hard enough to hurt much," remarked Andy.

"Huh! if half we've heard about that place is true, little danger of that," declared Seth. "Chances are he dropped with a splash into a bed of muck. I only hope he don't get drowned before help comes along!"

"Help! what sort of help can reach him there?" observed Fritz, solemnly; and then once again did those eight scouts exchange uneasy glances.

"As soon as we let them know in Beverly, why, sure they'll organize some sort of relief expedition. I know a dozen men who'd be only too glad to lend a helping hand to a lost aeronaut," Andy went on to say.

"Wherever do you suppose he came from, Paul?" asked Eben.

"Say, didn't you hear him say St. Louis?" demanded Seth. "Better take some of that wax out of your ears, Eben."

"Whee! that's a pretty good ways off, seems to me," the bugler remarked, shaking his head, as though he found the story hard to believe.

"Why, that's nothing to brag of," Seth assured him. "They have big balloon races from St. Louis every year, nearly, and the gas-bags drift hundreds of miles across the country. I read about several that landed in New Jersey, and one away up in Canada won the prize. This one met with trouble before it got many miles on its journey. And he wants us to report that the *Great Republic* is down; Anderson, he said his name was, didn't he, Paul?"

"Yes, that was it," replied the scoutmaster.

Paul seemed to be looking unusually grave, and the others realized that he must have something of more than usual importance on his mind.

"How about that, Paul," broke out Fritz, who had been watching the face of the patrol leader, "we're about eighteen miles away from home; and must we wait till we get there to start help out for that poor chap?"

"He might die before then," remarked Jotham seriously.

Again a strange silence seemed to brood over the whole patrol. Every fellow no doubt was thinking the same thing just then, and yet each boy hated to be the one to put it into words.

They had taken so much pride in the big hike that to even suggest giving it up, and just in the supreme moment of victory, as it were, seemed next door to sacrilege, and yet they could not get around the fact that it seemed right up to them to try and save that forlorn aeronaut. His life was imperiled, and scouts are always taught to make sacrifices when they can stretch out a hand to help any one in jeopardy.

Paul heaved a great sigh.

"Fellows," he said, solemnly, "I'm going to put it up to you this time, because I feel that the responsibility ought to be shared; and remember majority rules whenever the scoutmaster thinks best to let the troop decide."

"All right, Paul," muttered Seth, dejectedly.

"It's only fair that you should saddle some of the responsibility on the rest of the bunch," admitted Jotham, hardly a bit more happy looking than Seth; for of course every one of them knew what was coming; and could give a pretty good guess as to the consequences.

"That's a fact," added Fritz, "so out with it, Paul. When I've got a bitter dose to swallow I want to hurry, and get it over."

"It hurts none of you more than it does me," went on the scoutmaster, firmly, "because I had set my heart on winning that fine trophy; and there'll be a lot of people disappointed this afternoon when we fail to show up, if we do."

"Sure thing," grunted Seth, "I c'n see our friend, Freddy Rossiter, going around with that sickly grin on his face, telling everybody that he always knew we were a lot of fakirs, and greatly overrated; and that, like as not, even if we did show up we'd a been carried many a mile on some hay-wagon. But go on, Paul; let's have the funeral quick, so a feller c'n breathe free again."

"I'm going to put a motion, and every scout has a right to vote just as he thinks best. Only before you decide, stop and think what it all means, to that poor man as well as ourselves," Paul continued.

"Ready for the motion," mumbled Fritz, who looked as though he had lost his very last friend, or was beginning to feel the advance symptoms of sea sickness.

"All in favor of changing our plans, and trying to rescue the lost balloonist right now, say yes," the scoutmaster demanded, in as firm a tone as he could muster.

A chorus of affirmatives rang out; some of the boys were a little weak in the reply they made, for it came with an awful wrench; but so far as Paul could decide the response was unanimous.

He smiled then.

"I'm proud of you, fellows, yes I am," he declared heartily. "I think I know just what each and every one of you feels, and when you give up a thing you've been setting your minds on so long, and just when it looks as if we had an easy walk-over, I'm sure it does you credit. Some of the Beverly people may laugh, and make fun when we fail to turn up this afternoon; but believe me, when we do come in, and they learn what's happened, those for whose opinion we care will think all the more of us for doing what we mean to."

"Hope so," sighed Seth, who could not coax any sort of a smile to his forlorn looking face, "but because I talk this way, Paul, don't you go and get the notion in your head that if the whole thing depended on me I'd do anything different from what we expect to. There's such a thing as duty that faces every scout who's worthy of the name. For that he must expect to give up a whole lot of things he'd like to do. And you'll find that I can stand it as well as the next feller."

"P'raps when they know what happened, the committee'll be willing to give us a chance to make another try next week?" suggested Jotham.

"Good boy, Jotham, and a clever idea," cried Fritz.

Somehow the suggestion seemed to give every one a sensation of relief.

"I think myself that we'll be given another chance to show what we can do," was what Paul remarked. "We can prove that we had the victory about as good as clinched when this unexpected thing came along. And I know Mr. Sargeant will be pleased to hear that we gave up our chances of winning that trophy because a sudden serious duty confronted us."

"Then we're going to start right away to try and find the middle of Black Water Swamps - is that the idea, Paul?" inquired Seth.

"That's what it amounts to, it looks like, to me," replied the scoutmaster, as he stood there in the open road, looking long and steadily at the very spot where they had seen the last of the dropping balloon; just as though he might be fixing the locality on his mind for future use.

"Do we all have to go, Paul, or are you going to let several of us tramp along to Beverly?" some one asked just then.

"That depends on how you feel about it," was the answer the scoutmaster gave. "It won't do any good for a part of the patrol to arrive on time, because, you remember one of the rules of the game is that every member must fulfill the conditions, and make the full hundred miles hike. Do you want to go to town, while the rest of us are searching the swamps for the aeronaut, Eben?"

"I should say not," hastily replied the bugler.

"How about you, Noodles?" continued Paul.

"Nixey doing; me for der swamps, undt you can put dot in your pipe undt smoke idt," the one addressed replied, for there were times when the scouts, being off duty, could forget that Paul was anything other than a chum.

"Well," the patrol leader went on to say, laughingly, "I'm not going to ask any other fellow, for I see by the looks on your faces that you'd take it as an insult. So, the next thing to settle is where we'd better strike into the place."

Seth came to the front again.

"Well, you see, I talked a lot with that feller that got lost in there; and he told a heap of interesting things about the blooming old swamp, also where he always started into the same when trapping. You see, somehow I got a hazy idea in this silly head of mine that some time or other I might want to get a couple of chums to go with me, and try and see what there was in the middle of the Black Water Swamps."

"That's good, Seth," declared one of his mates, encouragingly.

"The smartest thing you ever did, barring none," added Jotham.

"It's apt to be of more or less use to us right now, and that's a fact," was the way Paul put it.

"I reckon," Andy remarked, looking thoughtfully at Seth, "that you could tell right now whether we happened to be near that same place. It would be a great piece of good luck if we could run across the entrance, and the trail your trapper friend made, without going far away from here."

"Let's see," continued Seth, screwing his forehead up into a series of funny wrinkles, as he usually did when trying to look serious or thoughtful, "he told me the path he used lay right under a big sycamore tree that must have been struck by a stray bolt of lightning, some time or other, for all the limbs on the north side had been shaven clean off."

"Well, I declare!" ejaculated Jotham.

"Then you've noticed such a tree, have you?" asked Paul, instantly, recognizing the symptoms, for he had long made a study of each and every scout in the troop, and knew their peculiarities.

"Look over yonder, will you?" demanded Jotham, pointing.

Immediately various exclamations arose.

"That's the same old blasted sycamore he told me about, sure as you're born," declared Seth, with a wide grin of satisfaction.

"The Beaver Patrol luck right in the start; didn't I say nothing could hold out against that?" remarked Fritz.

"Come along, Paul; let's be heading that way," suggested Jotham.

In fact, all the scouts seemed anxious to get busy. The first pang of regret over giving up their cherished plan had by this time worn away, and just like boys, they were now fairly wild to be doing the next best thing. They entered heart and soul into things as they came along, whether it happened to be a baseball match; a football scrimmage on the gridiron; the searching for a lost trail in the woods, or answering the call to dinner.

And so the whole eight hurried along over the back road, meaning to branch off at the point nearest to the tall sycamore that had been visited by a freak bolt from the thunder clouds, during some storm in years gone by.

Paul was not joining in the chatter that kept pace with their movements. He realized that he had a serious proposition on his hands just then. If so experienced a man as that muskrat trapper could get lost in Black Water Swamps and stay lost for two whole days, it behooved a party of boys, unfamiliar with such surroundings to be very careful in all they did.

But Paul had ever been known as a cautious fellow. He seldom acted from impulse except when it became actually necessary, in order to meet some sudden emergency; and then there were few who could do things more quickly than the patrol leader.

In a case of this kind, the chances were that they must take unusual precaution against losing their bearings; that is, they must feel that they had a back trail to follow in case forward progress became impossible, or inexpedient.

Paul had his theory as to the best way to accomplish such a thing; and of course it had to do with "blazing" trees as they went along. In this fashion all chances of making mistakes would be obviated; and if they failed to effect the rescue of the man who had dropped in the heart of the dismal morass at least the eight boys need not share his sad fate.

Leaving the road they now headed straight for the sycamore that stood as a land mark, and a specimen of the freaks of lightning. No sooner had they reached it than Paul's eyes were on the ground.

The others heard him give a pleased exclamation, and then say:

"It's all right, fellows; because here is a well beaten trail that seems to lead straight in to the place. And now, follow me in single file!"

CHAPTER XI

THE TRAIL IN THE SWAMP

When the eight scouts found that they were leaving solid ground, and actually getting to where little bogs surrounded them on almost every side, they had a queer feeling. Up to now none of them had ever had much experience in passing through a real swamp, because there were no such places nearer to Beverly than this one, and eighteen miles is quite too far for boys to walk on ordinary occasions, when seeking fun.

They looked around time and again, though none of them dared loiter, and Paul, as the leader, was setting a pretty good pace.

Just behind Paul came Seth. The scoutmaster had asked him to keep close at his heels, for since Seth had acquired more or less of a fund of swamp lore from the man who trapped muskrats for their pelts, in the fall and winter, if any knotty problems came up to be solved the chances were Seth would be of more use than any one of the other fellows.

Evidently they were in for some new and perhaps novel experiences. And there is nothing that pleases the average boy more than to look upon unfamiliar scenes, unless it is to run up against a bit of an adventure.

One thing Paul had made sure to fetch along with him when taking this big hike, and that was his little camp hatchet. Fritz had begged to be allowed to carry his old Marlin shotgun, under the plea that they might run across some ferocious animal like a wildcat, or a skunk, and would find a good use for the reliable firearm; but the scoutmaster had set his foot down firmly there.

But they would have to make numerous fires while on the way, and a little hatchet was apt to come in very handy.

And the feel of it in his belt had given Paul his idea about "blazing" the trees just as soon as they no longer had the trapper's path to serve them as a guide against their return.

It is a very easy thing to make a trail in this way; only care must always be taken to make the slices, showing the white wood underneath the bark, on that side of the tree most likely to be seen by the returning pilgrim. Great loss of time must result if one always had to go behind every tree in order to find the blaze that had been so carefully given, not to mention the chances of becoming confused, and eventually completely turned around.

That path twisted and turned in the most amazing and perplexing manner possible.

Although Paul had purposely warned the boys to try and keep tabs of the points of the compass as they passed along, in less than ten minutes after striking the swamp proper it is doubtful whether one of them could have told correctly just where the north lay, if asked suddenly; though by figuring it out, looking at the sun, and all that, they might have replied with a certain amount of accuracy after a while.

But then they felt sure Paul knew; and somehow or other they had always been in the habit of relying on the scoutmaster to do some of their thinking for them - a bad habit it is, too, for any boys to let themselves fall into, and one that Paul often took them to task for. They would cheerfully admit the folly of such a course, and promise to reform, yet on the next occasion it would be the same old story of depending on Paul.

"Path seems to be petering out a heap, Paul," remarked Seth, when another little time had crept along, and they had penetrated still deeper into the swamp, with a very desolate scene all around them, water surrounding many of the trees that grew there with swollen boles, such as always seems to be the case where they exist in swampy regions.

"Yes, I was thinking that myself," replied the other; "and it's about time for me to begin using my little hatchet, even if I don't happen to be George Washington."

"Let's stop for a breath, and listen," suggested Eben; "who knows now but what we might be nearer where the balloon dropped than we thought. P'raps we could even get an answer if we whooped her up a bit."

"How about that, Paul?" demanded Fritz, who could shout louder perhaps than any other boy in Beverly, and often led the hosts as a cheer captain, when exciting games were on with other school teams.

"Not a bad idea, I should say," was the reply, as the patrol leader nodded his head in approval. "Suppose you lead off, Fritz, and let it be a concerted yell."

Accordingly Fritz marshaled them all in a line, and gave the word. Such an outbreak as followed awoke the sleeping echoes in the swamp, and sent a number of startled birds flying madly away. Indeed, Jotham noticed a rabbit bounding off among the hummocks of higher ground; and Noodles afterwards declared that he had seen the "cutest little pussycat" ambling away; though the others vowed it must have been a skunk, and gave Noodles fair warning that if ever he tried to catch such a cunning "pussycat" he would be buried up to the neck until his clothes were fumigated.

"Don't hear any answer, do you, fellers?" remarked Seth, after the echoes had finally died away again.

Everybody admitted that there seemed to have been no reply to the shout they had sent booming along.

"Hope we didn't scare him by making such a blooming row," Seth went on to say.

"I'm bothered more by thinking that he may have been killed, or very badly hurt when the balloon fell down," Paul ventured to say.

The thought made them all serious again. In imagination they pictured that valiant fellow who had taken his life in his hands in the interest of sport, possibly lying there on the ground senseless, or buried in the slimy mud, which could be seen in so many places all around them. And it was far from a pleasing prospect that confronted those eight scouts, though none of them gave any sign of wanting to back out.

"Mebbe a blast from my horn would reach him?" suggested Eben.

"Suppose you try it, eh? Paul?" Fritz remarked.

"No harm can come of it, so pitch in Eben," the other told the troop bugler.

"And put in all the wind you c'n scrape together," added Seth.

Accordingly Eben blew a blast that could have been heard fully a mile away. He grew red in the face as he sent out his call; and doubtless such a sweet medley of sounds had never before been heard in that desolate looking place since the time of the ice period.

"No use; he don't answer; or if he does, we don't get it," Seth observed, in a disappointed tone.

Archibald Lee Fletcher

"Then the only thing for us to do is to go ahead," Andy proposed.

"Paul's getting his bearings again," remarked Eben.

"I wanted to make dead sure," the scoutmaster observed, with a glow of determination in his eyes. "You see, we tried to note just about where the balloon seemed to fall; and it takes a lot of figuring to keep that spot in your mind all the while you're turning and twisting along this queer trail. But I feel pretty sure of my ground."

"Huh! wish I did the same," said Seth, holding up one of his feet, and showing that he had been in black mud half way to his knee, when he made some sort of bad guess about the footing under him.

Apparently Paul was now ready to once more start out. But they saw him give a quick hack at a tree, and upon looking as they passed they discovered that he had taken quite a slice off the bark, leaving a white space as big as his two hands, and which could easily be seen at some distance off in the direction whither they were bound.

That was called a "blaze."

If Seth thought he was having his troubles, they were slight compared with those that attacked one other member of the little band of would-be rescuers.

Noodles, besides being a good-natured chap, was more or less awkward. Being so very stout had more or less to do with this; and besides, he had a habit of just ambling along in any sort of happy-go-lucky way.

Now, while this might not be so very bad under ordinary conditions, when there was a decent and level road to be traveled over, it brought about all sorts of unexpected and unwelcome difficulties when they were trying to keep to a narrow and crooked path.

Twice already had Noodles made a slip, and gone in knee-deep, to be dragged out by some of his comrades. And he was glancing around at the gloomy aspect with a look approaching *fear* in his eyes, just as though he began to think that they were invading a haunted region where respectable scouts had no business to go, even on an errand of mercy.

Such was the wrought-up condition of his nerves, that when a branch which some one had held back, and then let slip, came in contact with the shins of Noodles, he gave out a screech, and began dancing around like mad.

"Snakes! and as big as your wrist too! I saw 'em!" he called out, forgetting to talk in his usual broken English way, because of his excitement.

They had some difficulty in convincing him that it was only a branch that had caressed his ankle, and not a venomous serpent; for Noodles confessed that if he dreaded anything on the face of the earth it was just snakes, any kind of crawling varmints, from the common everyday garter species to the big boa constrictor to be seen in the menagerie that came with the annual circus visiting Beverly.

Again and again was Paul making good use of his handy little camp hatchet, and Seth took note of the manner in which the blazed trail was thus fashioned. It may be all very fine to do things in theory, but there is nothing like a little practical demonstration. And in all likelihood not one of these seven boys but would be fully able to make just such a plain trail, should the necessity ever arise. When one has *seen* a thing done he can easily remember the manner of doing it; but it is so easy to get directions confused, and make blunders.

Paul was not hurrying now.

A mistake would be apt to cost them dear, and he believed that an ounce of prevention is always better than a pound of cure. If they could avoid going wrong, it did not matter a great deal that they made slow progress. "Be sure you're right and then go ahead" was the motto of the famous frontiersman, Davy Crockett, and Paul had long ago taken it as his pattern too.

Besides, it paid, for any one could see that they were steadily getting in deeper and deeper. The swamp was becoming much wilder now; and it was not hard to realize that a man getting lost here, and losing his head, might, after his bearings were gone, go wandering at haphazard for days, possibly crossing his own trail more than a few times.

It seemed a lonesome place. Animals they saw none. Perhaps there might be deer in the outer portions, but they never came in here. Although the scouts saw no evidences that wild-cats lived in the swamp, they could easily picture some such fierce animal crouching in this clump of matted trees or back of that heavy bush, watching their passage with fiery eyes.

The scouts found their long staves of considerable use from time to time. Had Noodles for instance been more adept in the use of the one he carried he might have been saved from a whole lot of trouble. Perhaps this might prove to be a valuable lesson to the boy. He could not help but see how smartly the others kept themselves from slipping off the narrow ridge of ground by planting their staves against some convenient stump, or the butt of a tree, anywhere but in the oozy mud.

"Wait up for me!" Noodles would call out every little while, when he fell behind, for he seemed to have a horror lest he might slip into that horrible bed of mud, and be sucked down before his chums could reach him. "It iss nodt fair to leave me so far behindt der rest. How wouldt you feel if you rescued der argonaut, and lose your chump; dell me dot? Give eferypody a chance, and - mine gootness, I mighty near proke my pack dot time," for he had come down with a tremendous thump, when his feet slipped out from under him.

But as a rule boys are not apt to give a clumsy comrade much sympathy, and hence only rude laughter greeted this fresh mishap on the part of Noodles.

"Nature looked out for you when she saw what an awkward chap you were going to be, Noodles," called back Fritz. "You're safely padded all right, and don't need to feel worried when you sit down, sudden-like. If it was me, now, there might be some talking, because I'm built more on the jack-knife plan."

"Oh! what is that?" cried Eben, as a strange, blood-curdling sound came from a point ahead of them; just as though some unlucky fellow was being sucked down in the embrace of that slimy mud, and was giving his last shriek for help.

As the other scouts had of course heard the same thing, all of the detachment came to a sudden halt, and looking rather apprehensively at one another, they waited to learn if the weird gurgling sound would be repeated, but all was deathly still.

Archibald Lee Fletcher

CHAPTER XII

WHERE NO FOOT HAS EVER TROD

"Now whatever do you suppose made that racket?" demanded Seth.

"Sounded just like a feller getting drowned, and with his mouth half full of water. But I don't believe it could have been a human being, do you, Paul?" and Eben turned to the one in command of the troop.

"No, I don't," returned the scoutmaster, promptly. "More than likely it was some sort of a bird."

"A bird make a screechy sound like that?" echoed the doubting Eben.

"Some sort of heron or crane. They make queer noises when they fight, or carry on in a sort of dance. I've read lots of things about cranes that are hard to believe, yet the naturalists stand for the truth of the accounts."

Paul started off again, as though not dismayed in the slightest by the strange squawk, half human in its way. And his example spurred the others on to follow in his wake, so that once more they were making steady progress.

"I wouldn't care so much," grumbled Fritz, as he trailed along, "if only I had a gun along. But it's tough luck to be smooching through a place like this, where a sly old cat may be watching you from the branch overhead, and your trusty Marlin hanging on the nails at home."

"They say you always see plenty of game when you haven't got a gun; and so I guess we'll run across all sorts of things, from bobcats to alligators!" Paul went on to remark, whimsically, but there was one scout who chose to take his words seriously, and this was Noodles.

"What's that about alligators?" he called out from his place at the rear of the little procession. "Blease don't dell me now as we shall some reptiles meet up mit pefore we finish dis exblorations. If dere iss one thing I don't like, worser as snakes, dose pe alligators. I would go across der street to avoid dem. You moost some fun pe making when you say dot, Paul?"

"Sure I am, Noodles," replied the scoutmaster quickly, "because there are no alligators or crocodiles native to the state of Indiana. I believe they have a few lobsters over in Indianapolis, but they don't count. But the chances are we will run across some queer things before we get out of this place."

"What gets me," remarked Jotham, "is the way the thing came on us. Why, we'd just about said that we'd like to explore the old swamp, from curiosity if nothing else, when that balloon hove in sight, and settled down where we'd have to push right into the center of the place to find the man who was hanging to the wreck."

"Well, we had our wish answered on the spot, didn't we?" questioned the patrol leader, "and it came in such a way that we couldn't well back out. So here we are, up to our necks in business."

"I only hopes as how we won't pe up to our necks in somedings else pefore long," came a whine from the rear, that made more than one fellow chuckle.

Archibald Lee Fletcher

A number of times Paul stopped, for one reason or another. Now it was some little imprint of animal feet that had attracted his attention in the harder mud at the side of the narrow ridge he was following; then again he wanted to listen, and renew his observations.

Seth was watching him closely. Somehow he was reminded of that grizzled old carpenter whom he had observed, when the addition was being put to their house, and who, after measuring a board three blessed times, and picking up his saw, made ready to cut it in twain, when, possessed of an idea that he must not make a miscalculation, laid down his saw, and went to work to measure it for the fourth time!

Paul was not quite so bad as all that, but he did like to make sure he was right before taking a step that could not be recovered, once it was gone.

"There's one thing sure," Seth could not help remarking, after he had watched Paul for some time, and noted how confident the other seemed with every forward step that was taken.

"What might that be, Seth?" demanded Babe Adams, when the other paused.

"If that feller I talked with, the one that hunts muskrats around here in the season, had been just half as smart as Paul, he never would a lost hisself in the swamps, and come near starving to death."

"So say we all of us!" added Jotham.

"That's as neat a compliment as I ever had paid me, boys; though I hardly think I deserve it, yet. Wait and see if we get lost, or not. The proof of the pudding's in the eating of it, you know. Talk is cheap and butters no parsnips, they say. I like to *do* things. But honestly speaking, I believe we're getting through this place pretty smartly."

"But she keeps agettin' darker right along, Paul?" complained Noodles, taking advantage of a brief halt to pick up a stick and start to wiping the dark ooze from the bottom of his trousers.

"That only means we're pushing steadily in toward the center; and I'm beginning to lose my fear about getting there. Perhaps, after all, it may be an easy thing to put our feet where those of no other white man has ever trod."

Paul spoke with an assurance that carried the rest along with him. That had ever been one of his strongest points at school in the leadership of the class athletic and outdoor sports team.

It was getting more and more difficult for several of the scouts to follow their leader. The narrow ledge had been bad enough, but when it came to passing along slippery logs, with the water all around, and a bath sure to follow the slightest mishap, Eben's nerve gave way.

"If it's going to keep up like this, Paul, you'll have to drop me out, because I just can't do it, and that's a fact!" he wailed, as he clung with both hands and knees to an unusually slippery place, having lost his stick in making a miscalculation when trying to brace himself.

One of the other fellows recovered the staff, and then Eben was assisted across. Paul had been expecting something like this, and was not very much surprised. He felt pretty sure there was another who would welcome an order to stay there on that little patch of firm ground, and wait for the return of the rest.

"Well, I was just thinking of leaving a rear guard, to protect our line of communications," he proceeded to say, gravely, but with a wink toward Seth and Fritz, "and as it will be necessary for two to fill the position, I appoint Seth and Noodles to the honorable post. You will take up your position here, and if anybody tries to pass you by without giving the proper countersign, arrest him on the spot."

"Which spot, Paul?" asked Noodles, solemnly.

"Well, it doesn't matter, so long as you stay here and guard our line of retreat. And boys, keep your eyes on the watch for signals. Perhaps we may have to talk with you by smoke signs. So you can amuse yourselves by picking up some wood, and getting ready to start a smoky fire, only don't put a match to it unless we call you."

"All right, Paul," returned Eben, taking it all in deadly earnest, although the other fellows were secretly chuckling among themselves. "And then again, I've got my bully old bugle, in case I want to give you a call. Don't worry about Noodles; I'll be here to look after him."

"The blind leading the blind," muttered Seth as he turned his face away.

"There, you see now," broke in Fritz, "if we only had my gun along, Eben here could be a real sentry, and hold a feller up in the right way. Watch this second slippery log here, boys. You c'n easy enough push anybody into the slush if he gets gay, and refuses to give the password."

Then he in turn also followed after Paul, leaving the bugler and Noodles there, congratulating themselves that they could be doing their full duty by the enterprise without taking any more desperate risks.

And then when the six scouts had gone about fifty feet Eben was heard wildly shouting after them.

"Paul, O! Paul!" he was bellowing at the top of his voice.

"Well, what is it?" asked the scoutmaster.

"You forgot something," came the answer.

"What?"

"You didn't give us the password, you know; and how c'n we tell whether any fellers has it right, when we don't even know."

Paul just turned and walked on, laughing to himself; and those who followed in his footsteps were shaking with inward amusement. Either Eben had taken the bait, and gorged the hook, or else he was having a little fun with them, no one knew which.

However, all of them soon realized that Paul had done a clever thing when he thus coaxed the two clumsy members of the patrol to drop out of line, and allow those better fitted for coping with the difficulties of the slippery path to go forward; because it steadily grew worse instead of better, and neither Eben nor Noodles could have long continued.

Why, even Fritz began to feel timid about pursuing such a treacherous course, and presently he sought information.

"Don't you think we must be nearly in the heart of the old bog, Paul? Seems to me we've come a long ways, and when you think that we've got to go back over the same nasty track again, perhaps carrying a wounded man, whew! however we are going to do it, beats me."

Paul stopped long enough to give a tree a couple of quick upward and downward strokes with that handy little tool of his, and then glance at the resulting gash, as though he wanted to make sure that it could be seen a decent distance off.

"Well, that's a pretty hard question to answer," he replied, slowly. "In the first place, we don't know whether the man fell into the heart of the Black Water, or over by the other side. Fact is, we haven't come on anything up to now to settle the matter whether he fell at all."

"Great governor! that *would* be a joke on us now, wouldn't it, if we made our way all over this beastly place, when there wasn't any aeronaut to help? We'd feel like a bunch of sillies, that's right!" burst out Fritz.

"But we acted in good faith," Paul went on to say, positively. "We weighed the matter, and arrived at the conclusion that he had fallen somewhere in here; and we agreed, *all of us*, mind you, Fritz, that it was our duty to make a hunt for Mr. Anderson. And we're here on the ground, doing our level best."

"Ain't got another word to say, Paul," Fritz observed, hastily, "you know best; only I sure hope it don't get any worse than we find it right now. I never did like soft slimy mud. Nearly got smothered in it once, when I was only a kid, and somehow it seems to give me the creeps every time I duck my leg in. But go right along; only if you hear me sing out, stop long enough to give me a pull."

"We're all bound to help each other, don't forget that, Fritz," said Seth. "It might just as well be me that'll take a slide, and go squash into that awful mess on the right, or on the left. Don't know whether to swim, or wade, if that happens; but see there, you can't find any bottom to the stuff."

He thrust his long Alpine staff into the mire as far as it could go; and the other scouts shuddered when they saw that so far as appearances went, the soft muck bed really had no bottom. Any one so unfortunate as to fall in would surely gradually sink far over his head, unless he were rescued in time, or else had the smartness to effect his own release by seizing hold of a low-hanging branch and gradually drawing his limbs out of the clinging stuff.

Then they all looked ahead, as though wondering what the prospect might be for a continuance of this perilous trip which had broken up their great hike.

"I guess it's about time to make another try with a shout or so, Fritz," said Paul, instead of giving the order for an advance.

"All right, just as you say," returned the other, "we've come quite some distance since we made the last big noise; and if he's weak and wounded, yet able to answer at all, p'raps we might hear him this time. Line up here, fellers, and watch my hands now, so's all to break loose together."

It was a tremendous volume of sound that welled forth, as Fritz waved his hands upward after a fashion that every high school fellow understood; why, Seth declared that it could have been heard a mile or more away, and from that part of the swamp half way out in either direction.

Then they strained their ears to listen for any possible answer. The seconds began to creep past, and disappointment had already commenced to grip hold of their hearts when they started, and looked quickly, eagerly, at one another.

"Did you hear it?" asked Fritz, gasping for breath after his exertions at holding on to that long-drawn school yell.

"We sure did - something!" replied Jotham, instantly, "but whether that was the balloonist answering, Eben or Noodles calling out to us, or some wild animal giving tongue, blest if I know."

And then, why, of course five pair of eyes were turned on Paul for the answer.

CHAPTER XIII

THE OASIS IN THE SWAMP

"Was that another fish-eating bird like a crane, Paul?" asked Seth.

"Sounded more like a human voice," Jotham put in.

"And that's what it was, or else we're all pretty much mistaken," was the verdict of the scoutmaster.

They turned their eyes toward the quarter from whence the sound had appeared to come; and while some thought it had welled up just in a line with this bunch of bushes, or it might be a leaning tree, still others believed it had come straight up against the breeze.

Although there might be a few points difference in their guesses, still it was noticeable that on the whole they were pretty uniform, and pointed almost due east from the spot where they stood.

"How about the prospect of getting through there?" queried Jotham, anxiously.

"Huh! couldn't be tougher, in my opinion," grumbled Seth.

"But if you look far enough, boys," remarked Paul, "you can see that there seems to be some firmer ground over there."

"Well, now, you're right about that, Paul," interjected Fritz, "I was just going to say the same myself. Made me think of what an oasis in a desert might look like, though to be sure I never saw one in my life."

"Solid ground, you mean, eh?" said Babe Adams, gleefully, "maybe, now, we won't be just tickled to death to feel the same under our trilbies again. This thing of picking your way along a slippery ledge about three inches wide, makes me feel like I'm walking on eggs all the while. Once you lose your grip, and souse you go up to your knees, or p'raps your neck, in the nasty dip. Solid ground will feel mighty welcome to me."

"Do we make a bee line for that quarter, Paul?" asked Andy.

"I'd like to see you try it, that's what," jeered Seth. "In three shakes of a lamb's tail you'd be swimming in the mud. Guess we have to follow one of these crazy little hummocks that run criss-cross through the place, eh, Frank?"

"Yes, you're right about that, Seth; but I'm glad to say I think one runs over toward that spot; anyway, here goes to find out."

The young scoutmaster made a start while speaking, and the balance of the boys lined out after him.

"Keep close together, so as to help each other if any trouble comes," was what Paul called out over his shoulder.

"Yes, and for goodness sake don't all get in at once, or we'll be drowned. Think what an awful time there'd be in old Beverly, if six of her shining lights went and got snuffed out all at once. Hey, quit your pushin' there, Jotham, you nearly had me overboard that time."

"Well, I just *had* to grab something, because one of my legs was in up to the knee. Oh! dear, what a fine time we'll have getting all this mud off us," Jotham complained, from just behind.

But they were making pretty fair progress, all the same; and whenever any of the boys could venture to take their eyes off the faintly marked path they were following, long enough to send a quick look ahead, they saw that the anticipated haven of temporary refuge loomed up closer all the time.

At least this was encouraging, and it served to put fresh zeal in those who had begun to almost despair of ever getting across the acre of mud that lay between the spot where they had last shouted, and the Promised Land.

They were a cheery lot, taken as a whole; and what was even better, they believed in passing their enthusiasm along. So one, and then another, called out some encouraging words as the humor seized them.

Foot by foot, and yard by yard they moved along, Paul always cautious about venturing upon unknown ground; but finding a way to gain his end.

"Here's a little patch of solid ground, and we can rest up for a minute or so," was the welcome announcement that came along the line of toiling scouts, and of course brought out various exclamations of delight.

It was indeed a great relief to be able to actually stand upright once more, so as to stretch the cramped muscles in their legs. Some of the boys even started to dancing, though Seth scorned to do anything like this, and pretended to make all manner of fun of their contortions.

"Talk about them cranes doing funny stunts when they get together and dance," he remarked, "I guess, now, they haven't got anything on you fellers. Why, if anybody happened to see you carryin' on that way he'd sure believe the whole bunch had broke loose from some lunatic asylum. When I dance I like to have some style about it, and not just hop around any old way."

So Seth took it out in stretching his arms, and rubbing the tired muscles of his legs.

It was Jotham who made a discovery. In jumping around he had by chance wandered a dozen yards away from the rest, when he was heard to give vent to a cry; and the other boys saw him dart forward, as if to pick something up from the ground.

"What is it, Jotham?" several cried in an eager chorus; for their nerves had been wrought up to a high tension by all they had gone through, and they felt, as Seth aptly expressed it, "like fiddle strings keyed to next door to the snapping point."

For answer Jotham turned and came toward the rest. He was carrying some object in his hand, and seemed to regard it with considerable interest, as though he felt that he had made an important discovery.

As he reached the others he held it up before the scoutmaster; and of course all could see what it was.

"A piece of old yellow cloth!" exclaimed Seth, in disgust, "say, you made all of us believe that you'd run across something worth while."

"How about it, Paul?" appealed Jotham, turning to the one whom he fancied would be more apt to understand, "don't this tell a story; and ain't it a pretty good clue to run across?"

"I should say, yes," replied Paul, as he took the article in question in his own hands, and felt of it eagerly, "because, you see, Seth, this is really silk, the queer kind they always make balloons out of. And that ought to tell us we're on the right track. So you see it was an important pick-up, and ought to count one point for Jotham."

"Gee whittaker! you don't say?" ejaculated Seth, staring with considerable more respect at the foot of dingy yellow stuff which the scoutmaster was holding in his hands. "Well, if that's so, then I pass along the honors to Jotham. But if a piece of the bally old balloon fell right here, Paul, don't that tell us the wreck must a passed over where we're standing now?"

"Not the least doubt about that," asserted the confident Paul, "and I was just looking up to see if I could make out the course it took. Because it must have struck the top of a tree, to tear this piece loose."

"How about that one over yonder?" suggested Fritz, pointing as he spoke. "Looks to me like the top was broke some, and I just bet you now that's where the big gas-bag did strike first, when it started to drop in a hurry."

"Then following the course of the wind, which hasn't changed this last hour, it would be carried on straight east," Paul continued, logically.

"Sure thing," declared Seth, "and if you look close now, you'll glimpse where it struck that smaller bunch of trees just ahead, where we're going to land soon. And Paul, hadn't we better be trying our luck some more now? Guess all the boys must be rested, and if we've just *got* to do the grand wading act, the sooner we get started the better."

"First let's call out again, and see if we get any answer. It would cheer the poor fellow up some, if he happens to be lying there badly hurt; and if he does answer, we'll get our bearings better. Hit it up, Fritz!"

They always turned to Fritz when they wanted volume of sound. That appeared to be his specialty, the one thing in which he certainly excelled.

Of course there was little need of any great noise, now that they had reason to believe the object of their solicitude must be close at hand; but then boys generally have plenty of spare enthusiasm, and when Fritz gave the required signal they let out a roar, as usual.

"There, that was certainly an answering call!" declared Jotham, proudly.

"Sounded like he said just two words - 'help - hurry!'" spoke up Babe.

Somehow the rest seemed to be of about the same opinion, and the thought gave the scouts a strange thrill. Was the unfortunate aeronaut slowly bleeding to death, lying there amidst the bushes on that tongue of land? They had given up their dearly cherished plan in order to rescue him, and had undergone considerable in the line of strenuous work, so as to arrive in time, and now that they were so close to the scene of his disaster it would be too bad if they were held back until it was too late to do him any good.

"Can't we hit it up a little faster, Paul?" begged Andy, who was rather inclined to be impulsive, because of the warm Southern blood that flowed in his veins.

They had once more started on, and were really making pretty good progress; but when one gives way to impatience, it may seem that a fair amount of speed is next door to standing still.

Paul understood the generous impulse that caused the Kentucky boy to speak in this strain and while he knew that it was dangerous to attempt any swifter pace than they were then making, still, for once, he bowed to the will of the majority, and began to increase his speed.

All went well, for beyond a few minor mishaps they managed to get along. What if one of the scouts did occasionally slip off the wretched footing, and splash into the mud; a helping hand was always ready to do the needful, and the delay could hardly be noticed.

"There's the beginning of the firm ground just ahead!" Paul

presently remarked, thinking to cheer his comrades with the good news.

"Oh! joy!" breathed Jotham, who often used queer expressions, that is, rather odd to hear from a boy.

Seth was the more natural one of the two when he gave vent to his delight by using the one expressive word:

"Bully!"

In a couple of minutes at this rate they would have reached the place where the slippery trail merged into the more solid ground.

Perhaps some of the others may not as yet have noticed strange sounds welling up out of the bushes beyond, but Paul certainly did, and he was greatly puzzled to account for the same.

That singular growling could not be the wind passing through the upper branches of the trees, for one thing. It seemed to Paul more like the snarling of an angry domestic cat, several times magnified.

For the life of him he could not imagine what a cat would be doing here in the heart of the dreaded Black Water Swamps. Surely no hermit could be living in such a dismal and inaccessible place; even a crazy man would never dream of passing over such a terribly slippery ledge in order to get to and from his lonely habitation.

But if not a cat, what was making that angry snarling?

Paul knew next to nothing about balloons, but he felt pretty sure that even the escaping of gas could hardly produce such a sound - it might pass through a rent in the silk with a sharp hiss, but he could plainly catch something more than that.

And then his foot struck solid ground; with a sigh of relief he drew himself up, and turned to give a hand to Seth, next in line, if it was needed.

So they all came ashore, so to speak, and delighted to feel able to stand in a comfortable position once more.

No time now for stretching or dancing, with that ugly snarling growing constantly deeper, and more angry in volume. Forward was the word, and Paul somehow felt glad that they gripped those handy staves, tried and true, with which every scout in course of time becomes quite adept. They would come in good play should there be any necessity for prompt action.

"Follow me, everybody," said Paul, as he started off.

"Count on us to back you up!" Seth declared, from which remark the scoutmaster understood that by now the others must have caught those suspicious sounds, and were trying to figure out what they stood for.

It seemed as if with every forward step he took, Paul could catch them more and more plainly. Nor was the snarling sound alone; now he believed he caught a rustling of dead leaves, and something that might be likened to low muttered words, as though the speaker were being hard pressed, and had little breath to spare.

Then, as he pushed through the last fringe of bushes that interfered with his view, Paul found himself looking upon the cause of all these queer noises.

CHAPTER XIV

JUST IN THE NICK OF TIME

"Holy smoke! look at that, would you?" exclaimed Seth, who had been so close on the heels of the scoutmaster that he sighted the struggling objects ahead almost as soon as Paul did himself.

"It's a big wildcat!" echoed Jotham, with a suspicious tremor in his voice.

Indeed, the animal in question was a sight well calculated to give any one more or less reason to feel a touch of alarm.

Evidently she must be a mother cat, for a couple of partly grown kittens stood there in plain sight, with every hair on their short backs erected, and their whole appearance indicating that they were "chips off the old block," as Seth afterwards declared.

The wounded aeronaut sat there with a stick in his grasp. This he was wielding as best he could, to keep the angry animal at a distance, although his efforts were growing pitifully weaker, and only for the coming of the scouts he must have been compelled to throw up the sponge in a short time.

Evidently the wildcat had come upon him there after he had been dropped amidst the wreckage of his balloon. Whether it was her natural hatred for mankind that tempted the savage beast to attack the balloonist, or the scent of fresh blood from some of his scratches, it would be hard to say, possibly both reasons had to do with her action.

Just how long the scrimmage had been going on Paul could only guess; but he did know that the beast must have ripped the clothes partly off the aeronaut's back, and in turn he could see that one of the animal's eyes was partly closed, from a vigorous whack which the desperate man had given with his cudgel, no doubt.

Paul instantly made straight for the scene of commotion, never so much as hesitating a second. This was one of those emergencies spoken of before now, when the scoutmaster did not allow himself to pause and consider, but acted from impulse only.

The man saw him coming, and gave expression to his satisfaction in a weak hurrah. As for the cat, at first it seemed ready to try conclusions with the whole troop of Boy Scouts, for it turned on Paul with the ugliest glare in its yellow eyes he had ever seen.

Every fellow was shouting vigorously by now, and the volume of sound must have had more or less to do with settling the question. Besides, the pair of kittens seemed to have been frightened off with the coming of the scouts, having slid into the friendly bushes.

So the mother cat decided that after all she could yield gracefully to superior numbers - seven to one was pretty heavy odds, and those waving staves had an ugly look she did not exactly fancy.

But all the same there was nothing inglorious in her retreat; she retired in perfect good order, keeping her face to the foe, and continuing to spit and snarl and growl so long as she remained in sight.

Archibald Lee Fletcher

Several of the scouts were for following her up, and forcing the issue; but a word from Paul restrained them. He saw that the animal was furiously angry, and if hard pushed would undoubtedly make things extremely interesting for any number of fellows; flying into their midst, so that they could not well use their sticks, and using her sharp claws to make criss-cross maps across their faces.

Scratches from the claws of all carnivorous animals are dangerous. Blood poisoning is apt to set in, because of the fact that their claws are contaminated from the flesh of such birds or small game as have served them for a previous meal. And just then Paul had nothing along with him to prevent the possibility of such a dreadful happening taking place.

Seth in particular was exceedingly loth to give over. He looked after the vanishing wild cat, and shook his head in bitter disappointment. Only for his pride in obeying all orders that came to him from the scoutmaster, Seth very likely would have followed the cat, and probably rued his rashness when he had to call for help a minute or so later.

Meanwhile Paul had hurried to the side of the aeronaut, who raised his hand in greeting, while a smile broke over his anxious face.

"Welcome, my brave boys!" he exclaimed. "I never dreamed that you could ever get to me here, when I saw what a horrible sort of bog I had dropped into. And then, after that savage beast set on me I about gave myself up as lost. She kept walking around me, and growling for a long time before she made a jump. Oh! it was a nightmare of a time, I assure you. I've seen some scrapes before in my ballooning experiences, but never one the equal of this. I'm mighty glad to meet you all. But I'll never understand how you found me. After this I'll believe Boy Scouts can do about anything there is going."

Well, that was praise enough to make every fellow glow with satisfaction, and feel glad to know he wore the khaki that had won the sincere respect of this daring voyager of the skies.

"I hope you're not very badly hurt, Mr. Anderson?" Paul ventured, as he knelt at the side of the other.

"I don't believe it's serious, but all the same I'm pretty much crippled after all I've gone through with on this ill-fated trip. But I'm willing to exert myself to the limit in order to get out of this terrible swamp. You can't make a start any too soon to please me."

Paul drew a long breath. If it had been so difficult for active boys, used to balancing, and doing all sorts of stunts, to cross on those treacherous little hummock paths, how in the wide world were they ever going to get a wounded man out of this place?

He only hoped Mr. Anderson would prove to be the possessor of tenacious will power, as well as a reserve fund of strength; he would certainly have good need of both before he struck solid ground again, once the return journey was begun.

"Well, while my chums are getting their breath after our little jaunt, suppose you let me look at any cuts you've got, Mr. Anderson," he suggested, first of all, in a business-like way that quite charmed the aeronaut.

"What, you don't mean to tell me that you are something of a doctor as well as a leader of scouts?" he remarked, with evident pleasure, as he started to roll up one of the legs of his trousers, so as to expose his bruised ankle.

"I know just a little about medicine, enough to make the other fellows want me to take charge whenever they get hurt. Let me introduce my friends, sir."

And accordingly Paul mentioned his own name, and then in turn that of Andy, Babe, Jotham, Seth and Fritz; also stating that there were two more in the patrol whom they had left

Archibald Lee Fletcher

stranded about half way out of the swamp, to be picked up again on the return journey.

The pleased aeronaut shook hands heartily with each boy. He was experiencing a delightful revulsion of feeling, for all of a sudden the darkness had given way to broad daylight.

Paul on his part, after a superficial examination, was glad to find there was really nothing serious the matter. He had feared lest he might find a broken leg or even a few ribs fractured; but nothing of the kind seemed to be the case.

It was true that Mr. Anderson had a lot of black and blue places upon his person, and would doubtless feel pretty sore for some days to come, but really Paul could not see why he should not be able to keep company with his rescuers. He seemed to possess an uncommon share of grit; his determined defense against the savage wildcat proved that plainly enough; and on the whole, with what help the scouts might give on occasion, there was a fair chance of his getting out of the swamp inside of an hour or so.

"Now I'm ready to make a start, if you say the word," Paul observed, when perhaps five minutes had passed.

The gentleman had been helped to his feet. Trying the injured leg, he declared he believed he would be able to get along; even though he did make a wry face at the very moment of saying this.

Paul endeavored to explain to him what sort of work lay before them, passing along on such insecure footing.

"Well, I must get in touch with a doctor, and that as speedily as possible," remarked Mr. Anderson, "and I'll get out of this horrible place if I have to crawl every foot of the way on my hands and knees. But I don't imagine it's going to come to such a pass as that, yet awhile. I'm ready to take my first lesson, Paul, if so be you lead the way."

Already the aeronaut seemed to have taken a great fancy for the young scoutmaster; but then that was only what might be expected. Paul had led the relief expedition; and besides, there was something attractive about the boy that always drew people to him.

"Then please follow directly after me; and Seth, you fall in behind Mr. Anderson, will you?" Paul went on to say.

"Huh! hope you don't mean that the way you say it," grunted Seth, with a wide grin, "because, seems to me I've done nothing else but *fall in* ever since I got on the go. I've investigated nearly every bog along the line, and found 'em all pretty much alike, and not to my likin' one single bit."

But all the same, Seth felt proud of the fact that the scoutmaster had selected him for the post of honor; for he knew that, coming just behind the wounded balloonist, he would be expected to lend a helping hand at such times as Mr. Anderson experienced a slip.

Just the consciousness of responsibility was apt to make Seth much more sure-footed than before. It is always so; and wise teachers watch their chances to make boys feel that they are of some consequence. Besides, experiences goes a great way and Seth, having tested nearly all the muddy stretches along the way, had in a measure learned how to avoid contact with them again.

In another minute the boys and Mr. Anderson were on the move. No doubt, if that savage mother cat and her charges were secretly watching from a leafy covert near by, they must have been heartily gratified because the menacing enemy had seen fit to quit the oasis in the swamp, leaving the remnants of the wrecked balloon to be pawed over by the frolicsome kittens.

"I see that you are true scouts, for you have blazed the way as prettily as I ever saw it done, Mr. Anderson remarked presently.

"That was Paul's doing," spoke up Seth, not in the least jealous.

"Oh! it's the easiest thing to do that anybody ever tried," declared the scoutmaster without even looking back over his shoulder, for he needed his eyes in front constantly.

"So I understand," continued Mr. Anderson, "but then, it isn't everybody who can be smart enough to do the right thing at the right time."

"How do you make out, sir?" asked Paul, wishing to change the conversation, for, strange to say, he never liked to hear himself praised, in which he differed very much from the vast majority of boys.

"Getting along better than I expected, Paul," replied the wounded balloonist.

"It's only a question of time, then, before we pass out of the swamp," the other went on to say. "And as we've got our trail all laid out, and Seth knows the best places to try the mud, I guess we'll make it."

He was already thinking deeply and seriously. A sudden wild hope had flashed into Paul's brain, and if all went well he meant to put it up to the other scouts after a while.

When he looked at his watch he found that it was now just a quarter after ten; and doing some lightning calculating he believed they could be out of the morass, discounting any serious trouble, by another hour.

Then, supposing it took them forty-five minutes to get Mr. Anderson to the nearest farm house, even though they had to make a rude stretcher, and carry him, that brought the time to exactly noon.

Could they really do it, make the eighteen miles that still lay between themselves and the field at Beverly, where they were expected to show up some time that day, if they hoped to win the prize?

Some how the very possibility of being put upon his mettle gave Paul a thrill. He had no doubts concerning his own ability to finish the great hike within the specified space of time, before the sun had vanished behind the western horizon, but it was a grave question whether some of the other scouts could accomplish the task. There was Eben for instance, never a wonder when it came to running; and then fat Noodles would be apt to give out before two-thirds of those eighteen miles had been placed behind them.

But if there was a ghost of a chance Paul was determined to take advantage of it, and he believed that even the laggards would be keen to make the attempt, once he mentioned the subject to them.

And so they kept pushing steadily along, Mr. Anderson showing wonderful pluck, considering the pain he must be suffering all the while from his numerous bruises and cuts.

CHAPTER XV

ON THE HOME-STRETCH

Perhaps they were becoming experts at the game; or it might be that the going back over familiar ground made the job easier, since they could see each slippery place where an accident had happened on the outward trip, and thus grow additionally cautious.

Be that as it might, they made very few missteps on the return journey. Even Mr. Anderson managed to do himself great credit, and Seth did not have to help him up on the narrow ridge more than three or four times; nor were any of his mishaps of a serious nature.

In due time, therefore, they came in sight of the place where Eben and Noodles had been left. Their voices must have warned the pair that they were coming, for they could be seen shading their eyes with their hands to shut out the glare of the sun, as they watched the string of figures slowly picking a path through the sea of mud and water.

Apparently they must have counted an extra form among the muddy group; and just had to give expression to their satisfaction; for Noodles yelped excitedly, while Eben sent out a series of blasts from his bugle, which, upon examination, seemed to bear some faint earmarks to "Lo, the Conquering Hero Comes!"

And when they landed at this half-way stage in their tiresome journey, Mr. Anderson had to be introduced to the remaining members of the Beaver Patrol. He also insisted on shaking hands with them, as he had done all the others, and letting them know his now exalted opinion about the ability of Boy Scouts to do wonders, all of which was sweetest music in the ears of the pair who had been cheated out of their share of the honors in the actual rescue party.

When the march was resumed - and Paul hastened matters as much as he could in reason - Noodles and Eben insisted on asking many questions as to just how they had found the balloonist. They grew quite excited when they heard about the mother wildcat and her savage little kittens; and even indulged in speculations as to what a great time they would have had defending themselves, had a trio like that paid them a visit.

Oh! it was certainly wearisome work, keeping up that strained position of the leg muscles so long. Paul began to fear that they would never be able to accomplish the other task beyond, for he heard Noodles take his regular plunges every little while, and judged that the stout boy must by this time be a sight calculated to make his mother shed tears, if ever she saw him in such a state.

But all things must come to an end, and finally Seth gave a shout, like unto the glad whoop a wrecked mariner might set up at sight of land ahead.

"There's the place where we started in, Paul; yes, and I can see that queer tree at the spot the trapper's path ended, and the fun began!" he exclaimed.

"Bless you, Seth, for those comforting words!" called out Eben from close to the rear of the procession.

"One last little bulge, and then victory for us!" Fritz remarked, and if the gladness expressed in his voice could be taken as an index to the feelings of his heart, then the scout must be a happy fellow just then, when the clouds rolled away, to let the sun shine again.

Of course they made it without any more trouble than Noodles giving a last try at the friendly mud, as though wanting to really find out whether it did have any bottom down below or not. And when they took some sticks, and scraped the worst of the sticky mess off his face, Noodles promised to be a sight indeed. But Paul assured him that they would stop at the first spring they came across, in order to allow him to wash some of the stuff off.

"Ain't we a nobby looking bunch of scouts now, though?" remarked Fritz, as he glanced ruefully down at his muddy uniform; for as a rule the boy had been quite particular with his clothes, having reformed after joining the organization.

"It's too bad you were put to such straits to help me," declared Mr. Anderson, heartily, "and I mean to do everything in my power to keep you from feeling sorry that you gave up all chances of winning that beautiful trophy today. It was a shame, and I regret having been the unfortunate cause of it more than I can tell you."

"Oh! perhaps there might be a *little* bit of a chance left to us yet, sir," said Paul; at which every one of the other seven scouts pricked up his ears and crowded around.

"What d'ye mean, Paul, by sayin' that?" demanded Seth, his eyes opening wide as they became glued upon those of the scoutmaster, for knowing Paul as he did, he understood that the other must have some clever idea in mind.

"Yes, tell us what the scheme is?" pleaded Jotham, who had been really more disappointed of giving up the hike than any of the others; for he knew his mother, and a certain girl Jotham thought a good deal of, would be on the grandstand at the baseball grounds, waiting to cheer him as he passed by with his fellow scouts.

"It all depends on how long it takes us to get Mr. Anderson to the nearest farmhouse," Paul went on.

"Why, I remember seeing a house near the road just below where we left it to head for the swamp!" spoke up Fritz, eagerly, "and I guess we could carry him there in less'n half an hour if we had to."

At that the aeronaut spoke up.

"I protest. Please don't take me into consideration at all, boys," he hastened to say, "if there's the remotest chance for you to make your race, leave me right here, and start off. I'll find my way to the road, and then a farmhouse, where they'll take me in, and have me looked after. You've done wonders for me as it is, saved my life, I haven't the least doubt; and I'm going to remember it, you can depend, but I wish you'd let me take care of myself from now on."

But Paul shook his head. He understood the feeling that prompted the gentleman to speak in this vein; but he did not think Mr. Anderson was as well able to look out for himself as he would have them believe.

"We never do things by halves, sir," the scoutmaster said, steadily. "If you can hobble along with one of us on either side to help, we'll go that way; but if it's too much of an effort then I'll show you how smart we are about making a litter out of some of these saplings here on which we'll carry you."

Mr. Anderson looked pleased to hear Paul talk in this confident way; but would not listen to such a thing as treating him like a badly wounded man.

"Give me a shoulder to lean on, and I'm sure I can make it in decent time, boys," he declared.

So Paul ranged on his right, with sturdy Seth closing up on the left, and in this fashion they started out.

Archibald Lee Fletcher

The road was no great distance away, it will be remembered; and in less than ten minutes they had reached it. Then turning toward distant Beverly, they commenced to cover the ground they had previously gone over.

There was no mistake about the farmhouse, in due time it was reached. Their arrival quite excited the little household, for the men had come in from the fields to their midday meal.

Paul did not want to stop to explain matters; all that could be left to Mr. Anderson. The odor of dinner did make more than one of the scouts raise his eyebrows, and exchange a suggestive look with another; but they realized that every minute was precious to them now, and that they just could not stay long enough to sit and partake, though the farmer cordially invited them.

They did accept a few things to munch at as they walked along; and promised to send word to a certain address which the aeronaut gave them; and in fact Paul was to notify a committee by wire that disaster had overtaken the *Great Republic*, but that the aeronaut was safe, and wished the news to be communicated to his wife at a certain hotel in St. Louis.

Of course all of the boys knew what the new hope that had come to Paul amounted to. He had, with his customary carefulness, shown them in black and white figures just the number of miles that still remained uncovered, about eighteen in all, and then they figured out when the sun would be setting at Beverly.

"Six full hours, and then some," Seth had declared, with a look of contempt; as though he could see no reason why they should not come in on time easily. "Why, of course we c'n do it, and then not half try. Now, you'd think I'd be feeling stiff after that crouching work in the swamp. All a mistake. Never fitter in my life. I could start on a run right now, and cover some miles without an effort."

"Well, don't do it, then," advised Paul, "you know what happens to the racer who makes too big an effort in the start. Get warmed up to your work, and there's a chance to hold out. Better be in prime condition for the gruelling finish. That's the advice one of the greatest all-around athletes gives. So we'll start at a fair pace, and later on, if it becomes necessary we'll be able to run some."

Of course Paul was thinking while he said this of the weak links in the chain, no other than Eben and Noodles. The latter was a wretched runner at best. He could walk fairly well, after a fashion, as his work of the last three days proved; and by judicious management Paul hoped to coax Noodles along, mile after mile.

As they walked they munched the sandwiches provided at the farm house where Mr. Anderson had been left. Thus they killed two birds with one stone, as Paul put it - continued to cover a couple of precious miles while securing strength and comfort from the food.

Whenever a chance occurred Noodles would get to work again scraping some more dirt off his garments. Fritz often declared the county would prosecute him for leaving so many piles of swamp mud along the pike; but after each and every operation the stout boy declared that he felt in far better trim to continue the journey, and that at least pleased all hands.

"I'm beginning to hope, Noodles," remarked Jotham, "that by the time we get to Beverly you'll look half way decent, and not make the girls ashamed to own us as we march through the town to the music of a band, mebbe."

"Put I don't want to be owned py any girl as I knows; so what differences does idt make, dell me?" was all the satisfaction he got from the other; who was evidently more concerned about the cost of a new suit, all to be earned by his own individual exertions, than anything else.

When the first hour had passed, and they found that they had made four miles as near as could be told, some of the scouts were exultant, and loudly declared it was going to be as easy as falling off a log.

"A regular picnic, believe me!" declared Seth.

"Like taking candy from the baby!" Fritz affirmed.

"A walk-over!" was Babe's style of expressing his sentiments.

"Well, it will be that, if we ever get to Beverly green before the sun drops out of sight," laughed Paul.

He was only concerned about Noodles, truth to tell, for he knew that Eben, while no great athlete, had a reserve fund in his stubborn qualities, and would shut his teeth hard together toward the end, plodding along with grim determination. Noodles must be watched, and coddled most carefully, if they hoped to carry him with them over the line in time to claim the glorious trophy.

And that was really why Paul asked him to walk along with him, so that he could from time to time cheer the other up by a few words of praise that would make him believe he was showing great improvement in his stride. It could be seen by the way his eye lighted up that Noodles appreciated this flattery; he had a real jaunty air as he walked on, and even cast an occasional glance of commiseration back at the fellows less highly favored than himself.

Besides, Paul, as a careful manager, wished to husband a certain portion of the other's strength for the last five miles. He knew that must be the sticking time, when probably Noodles would declare he could not go another step, and endeavor to drop down beside the road to rest.

Now Paul knew how far being diplomatic went in an affair of this kind. He remembered hearing a story about two gentlemen on a hunting trip up in Maine, carrying a couple of air rubber mattresses for sleeping purposes, and wondering how they could get the two guides, one a native, and the other a Penobscot Indian, to blow them up every night.

So during the supper one of them got to comparing the chests of the two men, and exciting their rivalry as to which had the larger lungs. When he had them fully primed he said he had means of testing the matter, and brought out the twin air mattresses. Eagerly then the guides lay flat on their stomachs, and at the word started to blow like two-horse power engines. The first test was declared a *tie*; and after that the guides could hardly wait for night to come to try out their lungs against each other.

And with this story in his mind the young scoutmaster determined to play the two weak members of the Beaver Patrol against each other, having in view the benefit that would result from such keen rivalry.

First he talked to Noodles about Eben's awakening talent in the line of pedestrian feats; and soon had the stout boy affirming that he could beat the best efforts of the bugler without more than half trying.

Then Paul found a chance to arouse the ambition of Eben in turn, by hinting at what Noodles had boasted. Thus Paul presently had the two lads jealously watching each other. They did not come to any open rupture, because they were good fellows, and fast friends, but did Eben happen to take a notion to go up a little in the line in order to speak to one of the others, Noodles clung to him like a leech.

Indeed, Paul had to restrain the eager pair more than once, for they were so determined to excel the record, each of the other, that they gave evidences of even wanting to run.

By carefully nursing this spirit of emulation and rivalry the patrol leader believed he was assisting the cause, without doing either of his chums the slightest injury. It was a case of simply bringing out all there was in a couple of lads who, as a rule, were prone to give up too easily.

And so they kept tramping along the turnpike leading toward home, jollying each other, and every now and then, when resting for a bit, trying to remove some of the dreadful evidences of black mud from their usually natty uniforms and leggins.

"P'raps they'll think it the biggest joke going," remarked Seth, "when they get on to it that we've been in the Black Water Swamps, and I guess Freddy's crowd'll laugh themselves sick, like a lot of ninnies, but just wait till we tell what took us there, and show the card Mr. Anderson gave us, with his message for St. Louis on the back. Then it seems to me the laugh will be on them."

They took great consolation in remembering what a gallant piece of work they had been enabled to carry out since leaving Camp Alabama that morning. It would perhaps be carried far and wide in the papers, when Mr. Anderson's story was told, and reflect new glory on the uplifting tendency of the Boy Scout movement. People who did not understand what a wonderful lot of good was coming out of teaching growing lads to be able to take care of themselves under any and all conditions, besides being considerate for others, brave in time of danger, and generous toward even their enemies, would have their eyes opened.

And so it was a happy and merry parcel of scouts that plodded along the road leading to Beverly town that afternoon, as the sun sank lower and lower toward the West.

CHAPTER XVI

"WELL DONE, BEAVER PATROL!"

They had struck along the road leading from Scranton, and reached the well-known Jerusalem pike, of which mention has been frequently made in previous stories of this series.

As they passed the Stebbens and the Swartz farms the scouts gave a cheer that brought a waving of handkerchiefs from the windows of the houses, which were in plain sight of the road.

Far down in the west the glowing sun was sinking; but Paul had calculated well, and he knew that, barring accidents, they could easily make the town before the king of day passed from sight.

Once they had halted for a few minutes' rest, the last they expected to enjoy, and Paul had taken advantage of the opportunity to start a smoky fire; after which he and Seth, the signal sender of the patrol, used the latter's blanket to send a series of dense smoke clouds soaring upward at certain intervals.

One of the boys who expected to join the second patrol in the early fall, Steve Slimmons, would be on the lookout for this signal that would announce the coming of the weary column; and when he caught sight of the smoke waves it would be his duty to announce that, after all, the scouts had not fallen down in their brave attempt to win that glorious trophy; but were coming right along, and hoped to be on hand in due time.

Well, there would be a good many suppers delayed in and around Beverly on that night, some of the scouts told each other.

They could easily picture the green swarming with people, all watching up the road for the patrol to turn the bend, and come in sight, with unbroken ranks, having fulfilled the conditions of the hike to the letter.

There was no longer any need for Paul to excite the slumbering ambitions of either Eben or Noodles. Why, after they passed the crossroads where the ruins of the old blacksmith shop lay, in which they had held their first meetings, but which had been mysteriously burned down, some thought by mischievous and envious town boys - after they had gone by this well-known spot, and sighted the Scroggins farm beyond, every fellow had actually forgotten such a thing as fatigue. They held themselves up straight, and walked with a springy step that would go far toward indicating that a hundred miles in four days was only play for such seasoned veterans.

And now the outlying houses of the home town began to loom up. Why, to several of the boys it really seemed as though they must have been away for weeks. They eagerly pointed out various objects that were familiar in their eyes, just as if they had feared the whole map of the town might have been altered since they marched away on their little four day tramp.

Seth in particular was greatly amused by hearing this kind of talk. He had been away from home so much that the novelty of the sensation of coming back did not appeal to him, as it may have done to Eben and Jotham for instance.

"You fellers," said Seth, chuckling while he spoke, "make me think of the little kid that took a notion to run away from home, and wandered around all day. When night came along he just couldn't stand it any longer, and crept home. His folks knew what was up, and they settled on punishing him by not noticing him, or saying a thing about his being gone. The kid tried to ketch the attention of maw, but she was sewing, and kept right along, just like he'd been around all day. Then he tried dad; but he read his paper, and smoked his pipe, and never paid the least attention. That boy just couldn't understand it. There he'd been away from home a whole year it seemed to him, since morning, and yet nobody seemed to bother the least bit, or make a fuss over him. And when he couldn't get a rise from anybody, he saw the family pussy sittin' by the fire. 'Oh!' he says, says he, 'I see you've still got the same old cat you had when I went away!'"

Even Eben and Noodles laughed at that. They knew the joke was on them; but just at that moment both were feeling too happy to take offense at anything.

"There's the church steeple!" cried Babe.

"Yes, you're so tall you c'n see things long before the rest of us do," declared Jotham, not maliciously, but with the utmost good humor, for he knew that in a very short time now he would see his dear little mother, proudly watching him march past; and perhaps also discover a tiny web of a handkerchief waving from the pretty hand of a certain little girl he knew; and the thought made Jotham very happy.

"Listen! ain't that boys shouting?" demanded Seth.

"Just what it is now," replied Andy. "They've got scouts at the bend of the road, and know we're coming."

"We've done what we set out to do, fellers!" cried Seth, gloatingly.

"And the trophy belongs to us; for right now we're in Beverly town, and there's the blessed old sun still half an hour high," Fritz observed with pardonable pride in his voice.

Archibald Lee Fletcher

"And think of us getting that balloon man safe out of the Black Water Swamps; yes, and going to the middle of the patch, something that they say nobody ever did before! That's going to be a big feather in our caps, believe me," Seth went on to say, as he took a glance down at his stained khaki trousers and leggins.

Paul gave his little command one last look over, for they were now at the bend, and in another minute would come under the eyes of the dense crowd which, from all the signs that came to his ears, he felt sure had gathered to welcome the marching patrol home again after their long hike.

Then the curve in the road was reached; a dozen more steps and they turned it, to see the green fairly black with people, who waved their hats and handkerchiefs, and shouted, until it seemed to the proud scouts that the very foundations of the heavens must tremble under the roaring sound.

Chief Henshall was there, together with several of his men, keeping an avenue open along which the khaki-clad boys were to march, to a spot in front of the grand stand, where the generous donor of the trophy, together with a committee of prominent citizens of Beverly, waited to receive them.

It was perhaps the proudest moment in the lives of those eight boys when Paul, replying to the little speech which accompanied the passing of the silver cup, thanked Mr. Sargeant and the committee for the great interest taken in the formation of Beverly Troop; and in a few words explained just why he and his comrades came so near being unable to fulfill the obligations governing the hike.

When Mr. Sargeant read aloud the message which the wrecked balloonist was wiring to St. Louis, in which he declared that he owed his very life to the daring of the Boy Scouts, who had penetrated to the very center of the Black Water Swamps in order to rescue him, such a din of cheering as broke out had never been heard in Beverly since that never-to-be-forgotten day when the baseball nine came up from behind in the ninth inning, and clinched the victory that gave them the high school championship of the county for that year.

But the boys now began to realize that they were, as Seth expressed it, "some tired," and they only too willingly allowed their folks to carry them off home, to get washed up, and partake of a good meal. But no matter what each scout may have secretly thought when he sat down to a white tablecloth, with silver, and china, and polished glass around him, he stoutly avowed that nothing could equal the delight of a camp-fire, tin cups and platters, and simple camp fare, flanked by an appetite that was keener than anything ever known at home.

This work of four days was likely to long remain the banner achievement of the Beaver Patrol lads; but the vacation period still held out a few weeks further enjoyment, and it may be readily understood that such wide-awake fellows would be sure to hatch up more or less excitement before the call came to go back to school duties.

That this proved to be the case can be understood from the fact that another volume follows this story, bearing the significant title of "The Boy Scouts' Woodcraft Lesson; or, Proving Their Mettle in the Field." And the young reader who has become interested in the various doings of the scouts belonging to the Beaver Patrol can find in the pages of that book further accounts of what Acting Scoutmaster Paul Prentice and his seven valorous chums started out to accomplish, in order to prove that the education of a Boy Scout brings out the best there is in him, under any and all conditions.

Archibald Lee Fletcher

Choose from Thousands of 1stWorldLibrary Classics By

A. M. Barnard	C. M. Ingleby	Elizabeth Gaskell
Ada Leverson	Carolyn Wells	Elizabeth McCracken
Adolphus William Ward	Catherine Parr Traill	Elizabeth Von Arnim
Aesop	Charles A. Eastman	Ellem Key
Agatha Christie	Charles Amory Beach	Emerson Hough
Alexander Aaronsohn	Charles Dickens	Emilie F. Carlen
Alexander Kielland	Charles Dudley Warner	Emily Dickinson
Alexandre Dumas	Charles Farrar Browne	Enid Bagnold
Alfred Gatty	Charles Ives	Enilor Macartney Lane
Alfred Ollivant	Charles Kingsley	Erasmus W. Jones
Alice Duer Miller	Charles Klein	Ernie Howard Pie
Alice Turner Curtis	Charles Hanson Towne	Ethel May Dell
Alice Dunbar	Charles Lathrop Pack	Ethel Turner
Allen Chapman	Charles Romyn Dake	Ethel Watts Mumford
Ambrose Bierce	Charles Whibley	Eugenie Foa
Amelia E. Barr	Charles Willing Beale	Eugene Wood
Amory H. Bradford	Charlotte M. Braeme	Eustace Hale Ball
Andrew Lang	Charlotte M. Yonge	Evelyn Everett-green
Andrew McFarland Davis	Charlotte Perkins Stetson	Everard Cotes
Andy Adams	Clair W. Hayes	F. H. Cheley
Anna Alice Chapin	Clarence Day Jr.	F. J. Cross
Anna Sewell	Clarence E. Mulford	F. Marion Crawford
Annie Besant	Clemence Housman	Federick Austin Ogg
Annie Hamilton Donnell	Confucius	Ferdinand Ossendowski
Annie Payson Call	Coningsby Dawson	Francis Bacon
Annie Roe Carr	Cornelis DeWitt Wilcox	Francis Darwin
Annonaymous	Cyril Burleigh	Frances Hodgson Burnett
Anton Chekhov	D. H. Lawrence	Frances Parkinson Keyes
Arnold Bennett	Daniel Defoe	Frank Gee Patchin
Arthur Conan Doyle	David Garnett	Frank Harris
Arthur M. Winfield	Dinah Craik	Frank Jewett Mather
Arthur Ransome	Don Carlos Janes	Frank L. Packard
Arthur Schnitzler	Donald Keyhoe	Frank V. Webster
Atticus	Dorothy Kilner	Frederic Stewart Isham
B.H. Baden-Powell	Dougan Clark	Frederick Trevor Hill
B. M. Bower	Douglas Fairbanks	Frederick Winslow Taylor
B. C. Chatterjee	E. Nesbit	Friedrich Kerst
Baroness Emmuska Orczy	E.P.Roe	Friedrich Nietzsche
Baroness Orczy	E. Phillips Oppenheim	Fyodor Dostoyevsky
Basil King	Earl Barnes	G.A. Henty
Bayard Taylor	Edgar Rice Burroughs	G.K. Chesterton
Ben Macomber	Edith Van Dyne	Gabrielle E. Jackson
Bertha Muzzy Bower	Edith Wharton	Garrett P. Serviss
Bjornstjerne Bjornson	Edward Everett Hale	Gaston Leroux
Booth Tarkington	Edward J. O'Biren	George A. Warren
Boyd Cable	Edward S. Ellis	George Ade
Bram Stoker	Edwin L. Arnold	Geroge Bernard Shaw
C. Collodi	Eleanor Atkins	George Durston
C. E. Orr	Eliot Gregory	George Ebers

George Eliot
George Gissing
George MacDonald
George Meredith
George Orwell
George Sylvester Viereck
George Tucker
George W. Cable
George Wharton James
Gertrude Atherton
Gordon Casserly
Grace E. King
Grace Gallatin
Grace Greenwood
Grant Allen
Guillermo A. Sherwell
Gulielma Zollinger
Gustav Flaubert
H. A. Cody
H. B. Irving
H.C. Bailey
H. G. Wells
H. H. Munro
H. Irving Hancock
H. Rider Haggard
H. W. C. Davis
Haldeman Julius
Hall Caine
Hamilton Wright Mabie
Hans Christian Andersen
Harold Avery
Harold McGrath
Harriet Beecher Stowe
Harry Castlemon
Harry Coghill
Harry Houidini
Hayden Carruth
Helent Hunt Jackson
Helen Nicolay
Hendrik Conscience
Hendy David Thoreau
Henri Barbusse
Henrik Ibsen
Henry Adams
Henry Ford
Henry Frost
Henry James
Henry Jones Ford
Henry Seton Merriman
Henry W Longfellow
Herbert A. Giles

Herbert Carter
Herbert N. Casson
Herman Hesse
Hildegard G. Frey
Homer
Honore De Balzac
Horace B. Day
Horace Walpole
Horatio Alger Jr.
Howard Pyle
Howard R. Garis
Hugh Lofting
Hugh Walpole
Humphry Ward
Ian Maclaren
Inez Haynes Gillmore
Irving Bacheller
Isabel Hornibrook
Israel Abrahams
Ivan Turgenev
J.G.Austin
J. Henri Fabre
J. M. Barrie
J. Macdonald Oxley
J. S. Fletcher
J. S. Knowles
J. Storer Clouston
Jack London
Jacob Abbott
James Allen
James Andrews
James Baldwin
James Branch Cabell
James DeMille
James Joyce
James Lane Allen
James Lane Allen
James Oliver Curwood
James Oppenheim
James Otis
James R. Driscoll
Jane Austen
Jane L. Stewart
Janet Aldridge
Jens Peter Jacobsen
Jerome K. Jerome
John Burroughs
John Cournos
John F. Kennedy
John Gay
John Glasworthy

John Habberton
John Joy Bell
John Kendrick Bangs
John Milton
John Philip Sousa
Jonas Lauritz Idemil Lie
Jonathan Swift
Joseph A. Altsheler
Joseph Carey
Joseph Conrad
Joseph E. Badger Jr
Joseph Hergesheimer
Joseph Jacobs
Jules Vernes
Julian Hawthrone
Julie A Lippmann
Justin Huntly McCarthy
Kakuzo Okakura
Kenneth Grahame
Kenneth McGaffey
Kate Langley Bosher
Kate Langley Bosher
Katherine Cecil Thurston
Katherine Stokes
L. A. Abbot
L. T. Meade
L. Frank Baum
Latta Griswold
Laura Dent Crane
Laura Lee Hope
Laurence Housman
Lawrence Beasley
Leo Tolstoy
Leonid Andreyev
Lewis Carroll
Lewis Sperry Chafer
Lilian Bell
Lloyd Osbourne
Louis Hughes
Louis Tracy
Louisa May Alcott
Lucy Fitch Perkins
Lucy Maud Montgomery
Luther Benson
Lydia Miller Middleton
Lyndon Orr
M. Corvus
M. H. Adams
Margaret E. Sangster
Margret Howth
Margaret Vandercook

Margret Penrose	Rex E. Beach	Thomas H. Huxley
Maria Edgeworth	Richard Harding Davis	Thomas Hardy
Maria Thompson Daviess	Richard Jefferies	Thomas More
Mariano Azuela	Richard Le Gallienne	Thornton W. Burgess
Marion Polk Angellotti	Robert Barr	U. S. Grant
Mark Overton	Robert Frost	Valentine Williams
Mark Twain	Robert Gordon Anderson	Various Authors
Mary Austin	Robert L. Drake	Vaughan Kester
Mary Catherine Crowley	Robert Lansing	Victor Appleton
Mary Cole	Robert Lynd	Victoria Cross
Mary Hastings Bradley	Robert Michael Ballantyne	Virginia Woolf
Mary Roberts Rinehart	Robert W. Chambers	Wadsworth Camp
Mary Rowlandson	Rosa Nouchette Carey	Walter Camp
M. Wollstonecraft Shelley	Rudyard Kipling	Walter Scott
Maud Lindsay	Samuel B. Allison	Washington Irving
Max Beerbohm	Samuel Hopkins Adams	Wilbur Lawton
Myra Kelly	Sarah Bernhardt	Wilkie Collins
Nathaniel Hawthrone	Sarah C. Hallowell	Willa Cather
Nicolo Machiavelli	Selma Lagerlof	Willard F. Baker
O. F. Walton	Sherwood Anderson	William Dean Howells
Oscar Wilde	Sigmund Freud	William le Queux
Owen Johnson	Standish O'Grady	W. Makepeace Thackeray
P.G. Wodehouse	Stanley Weyman	William W. Walter
Paul and Mabel Thorne	Stella Benson	William Shakespeare
Paul G. Tomlinson	Stella M. Francis	Winston Churchill
Paul Severing	Stephen Crane	Yei Theodora Ozaki
Percy Brebner	Stewart Edward White	Yogi Ramacharaka
Peter B. Kyne	Stijn Streuvels	Young E. Allison
Plato	Swami Abhedananda	Zane Grey
R. Derby Holmes	Swami Parmananda	
R. L. Stevenson	T. S. Ackland	
R. S. Ball	T. S. Arthur	
Rabindranath Tagore	The Princess Der Ling	
Rahul Alvares	Thomas A. Janvier	
Ralph Bonehill	Thomas A Kempis	
Ralph Henry Barbour	Thomas Anderton	
Ralph Victor	Thomas Bailey Aldrich	
Ralph Waldo Emmerson	Thomas Bulfinch	
Rene Descartes	Thomas De Quincey	
Rex Beach	Thomas Dixon	

www.ingramcontent.com/pod-product-compliance
Lightning Source LLC
Chambersburg PA
CBHW020505100426
42813CB00030B/3126/J

* 9 7 8 1 4 2 1 8 2 3 1 8 8 *